INDEX

ABOUT THE AUTHOR 6

FOREWORD 8

Objectives of the Book 10

The Importance of Behavioral Finance in Today's World 12

PART I: THE LEGACY OF TRADITIONAL FINANCE 14

Origins and Foundations of Traditional Finance 14

Basic Assumptions of Traditional Finance 14

The Efficient Market Hypothesis 19

Classical Models: CAPM and the Rational Expectations Hypothesis 21

Market Anomalies 24

Criticism of Anomalies 26

Incorporating Anomalies into Hybrid Models 27

Challenges to the Rational Behavior Hypothesis 29

The Resilience of the Rational Hypothesis in Certain Contexts. 33

Interdisciplinary Explanations for the Failures of the Rational Hypothesis 34

PART II: THE BIRTH OF BEHAVIORAL FINANCE 37

Psychology Meets Finance 37

The Pioneers: Kahneman, Tversky, and Thaler 37

Decisions Under Uncertainty: Prospect Theory 38

Cognitive and Emotional Biases 39

R. Shiller, Irrational Exuberance, and Narratives 42

New Generations of Researchers: An Evolving Legacy 44

Neuroscience Meets Finance 45

Reason and Emotion: Two Sides of the Same Coin 46

The Role of Somatic Markers 46

Additional Neuroscience Topics 47

Case Studies: When Behavior Changed Markets 49

The Dot-Com Bubble 50

The Subprime Crisis 52

The Volatility of Cryptocurrencies 55

Other Major Historical Bubbles 57

PART III: THE PRESENT OF BEHAVIORAL FINANCE 60
Current Tools and Applications 60

Behavioral Alpha: How Managers Leverage Behavior 60

Designing Nudges in Financial Markets 66

The Role of Technology in Behavioral Finance 71

    Big Data and Behavioral Analysis 71

    Predictive Models with Artificial Intelligence 77

    Investor Sentiment Index 82

Cryptocurrencies and Blockchain: Hype or Real Transformation? 87

    Tokenized Finance 88

    Market Sentiment and Volatility 89

    Behavioral Decisions in Decentralized Environments 91

PART IV: THE FUTURE OF BEHAVIORAL FINANCE 93

AI as an Architect of Financial Behavior 93

    Emotional Algorithms 93

    Personalizing Financial Strategies with AI 100

Towards a New Paradigm: Cognitive Finance 105

    AI and Neuroeconomics 105

    The Impact of Automated Decisions on Behavior 111

Ethics and Regulation in an Automated Financial World 113

    Risks of Behavior Manipulation 114

    Regulatory Challenges at the Convergence of AI and Finance 115

PART V: FROM THEORY TO PRACTICE: REAL-WORLD APPLICATIONS 119

    Investor Behavior in Real Scenarios 119

    Designing Behavioral Strategies for Investors and Companies 122

    Simulations and Learning Tools 125

    Real Case Studies and Practical Simulations 129

    Ethics and Responsibility in Designing Behavioral Strategies . 131

    Recommendations for Practitioners and Educators 134

CONCLUSION 139

    Final Reflections and the Role of Behavior in the Finance of Tomorrow 139

APPENDICES 142

Glossary of Key Terms 142

Bibliography and Recommended Resources 149

ABOUT THE AUTHOR

Sebastián Laza is an Argentine economist renowned across South America for his contributions to the fields of neuroeconomics, behavioral finance, and the economics of behavior. With a distinguished academic and professional career, Laza has focused his work on unraveling how emotions, cognitive biases, and expectations shape the financial and economic decisions of individuals, businesses, and governments.

Hailing from Mendoza, Argentina, Laza has successfully combined his theoretical knowledge with a sharp analysis of local and global economic dynamics. He is the author of two previous books that have become milestones in his field: *Neuroeconomics: The New Science of Decisions* (2019), a pioneering exploration of how the human brain influences economic decision-making, and *The Economics of Emotions* (2021, co-authored with Venezuelan economist Marisela Cuevas Sarmiento), a work that examines how emotions shape economic behavior in an increasingly complex world. Both titles, published by Editorial Libryco, have become key references for academics and professionals alike.

In addition to his research endeavors, Laza is a passionate educator and speaker, celebrated for his ability to make complex economic concepts accessible to diverse audiences. In this new book, he invites readers on a journey that spans from the foundations of traditional finance to the transformations brought about by behavioral sciences and artificial intelligence in the realm of finance. His interdisciplinary approach reflects not only his technical expertise but also his commitment to understanding and explaining economics as a profoundly human science.

FOREWORD

The Transformation of Finance: A Journey from Reason to Behavior

For decades, finance has been regarded as a domain of precise numbers, mathematical theories, and rational models. From the Capital Asset Pricing Model (CAPM) to the Efficient Market Hypothesis (EMH), the belief in investor rationality and market efficiency has traditionally dominated academic and practical thinking. However, reality has always been far more complex. Markets are not cold mechanical cogs but living organisms driven by emotions, intuitions, and often irrationalities.

This book arises from the need to explore this other dimension of finance: the human side. Why do investors tend to panic-sell during market downturns? What causes a financial bubble to inflate until it bursts? Why do we cling to a losing investment rather than accept a loss? Questions like these cannot be answered solely with numbers; they require an examination of the human mind and its behavior.

The union of psychology with finance, known as behavioral finance, has revolutionized our understanding of the financial world. Visionary pioneers like Daniel Kahneman, Amos Tversky, Robert Shiller, and Richard Thaler have shed light on the emotional and cognitive forces that shape our economic decisions. This book will take you on a journey from the fundamentals of traditional finance to behavioral finance, explaining how biases and emotions challenge traditional models.

However, we will not stop there. We are entering an era where artificial intelligence (AI) and big data are reshaping the rules of the game. AI can not only detect patterns in markets but also in human behavior, enabling the design of hyper-personalized financial strategies based on emotional analysis. What does this mean for the future of finance? Are we facing a tool for improvement or a Pandora's box with ethical and social implications?

This book does not aim to offer definitive answers but rather invites you on a journey of discovery. We will explore how traditional finance has evolved, how biases, emotions, and bounded rationality shape critical decisions, and how technology is transforming the financial landscape. The reader will find both theory and practical cases here, from historical bubbles to cryptocurrencies, as well as the impact of AI on financial management.

Human behavior is not an anomaly in markets; it is their core. Understanding it not only makes us better investors but also more aware decision-makers in an increasingly complex and connected world. I hope this book sparks your curiosity and inspires you to view finance from a new perspective, where psychology, behavior, and technology converge to define the future.

Welcome to this amazing journey through modern behavioral finance.

Objectives of the Book

General Objective

Explore the evolution of finance from its traditional focus to the integration of psychology, behavioral biases, and artificial intelligence, providing readers with a deep and practical understanding of how these elements are transforming the financial world.

Specific Objectives

1. **Educate on the Fundamentals of Traditional Finance:**

   Explain the key theories and principles historically guiding financial decisions, from the efficient market hypothesis to classical quantitative models.

2. **Introduce Concepts of Behavioral Finance:**

   Identify the main cognitive, emotional, and social biases affecting financial decisions, illustrating how they challenge the rationality assumptions of traditional finance.

3. **Connect Finance with Psychology:**

   Demonstrate how findings from psychology, behavioral economics, and neuroscience enrich our understanding of human behavior in markets.

4. **Analyze Real-Life Examples and Case Studies:**

   Examine financial phenomena such as bubbles, crises, and investment trends from a behavioral perspective, offering concrete and applicable lessons.

5. **Explore the Role of Artificial Intelligence in Finance:**

Describe how AI is revolutionizing finance through big data analysis, personalized strategies, and modeling human behavior.

6. **Reflect on the Future of Finance:**

   Anticipate how integrating technology and behavioral sciences will shape the financial markets of tomorrow, addressing ethical challenges and innovative opportunities.

7. **Promote More Conscious Decision-Making:**

   Help readers identify and mitigate their biases, enhancing their ability to make more informed and balanced financial decisions.

Target Audience

This book is aimed at:

- Financial professionals seeking a better understanding of human decision-making in markets.
- Students and academics interested in finance, behavioral economics, and psychology.
- Investors and wealth managers aiming to optimize their strategies in a changing environment.
- General audiences curious about how the human mind and technology influence the financial world.

The Importance of Behavioral Finance in Today's World

In an increasingly interconnected and complex world, understanding human behavior has become a necessity rather than a luxury. Behavioral finance, by placing the individual at the center of analysis, offers a more realistic and comprehensive view of how financial markets operate and how economic decisions are made.

An Era of Change and Challenges

Recent events, from global financial crises to phenomena like the rise of cryptocurrencies, have shown that traditional rationality assumptions do not always explain reality. Fear, greed, overconfidence, and other biases play crucial roles in markets. Behavioral finance not only explains these phenomena but also provides tools to anticipate and manage them.

A Human-Centered Approach

Unlike traditional finance, which assumes perfectly informed and rational economic agents, behavioral finance acknowledges that financial decisions are influenced by emotions, past experiences, and cognitive biases. This allows for the analysis of real-world problems, such as why investors tend to sell in panic or hold onto losing assets for too long.

Practical Applications

Today, behavioral finance is applied in various areas:

- **Investment Management:** Designing portfolios that account not only for expected returns but also for emotional risk tolerance.
- **Financial Education:** Helping individuals identify and mitigate biases that affect economic decisions.

- **Public Policies:** Designing interventions that encourage responsible financial behaviors, such as saving or retirement planning.
- **Businesses:** Understanding how biases influence executive decisions and consumer behavior.

Technology as an Ally

The rise of artificial intelligence and big data has taken behavioral finance to a new level. These technologies allow real-time analysis of behavioral patterns, development of personalized strategies, and prediction of emotional responses in uncertain situations. This combination of human and technological analysis is redefining how we understand and manage financial markets.

A Tool to Navigate Uncertainty

In a global environment marked by volatility, behavioral finance provides a framework for understanding the impact of emotions and biases on decision-making. Beyond markets, this approach helps us make more informed, conscious, and balanced decisions in our daily lives.

Behavioral finance is not merely an extension of traditional theories but a way to rethink our relationship with money, risk, and uncertainty. In a constantly evolving world, its relevance will only continue to grow.

PART I: THE LEGACY OF TRADITIONAL FINANCE

Origins and Foundations of Traditional Finance

Traditional finance has been the cornerstone of financial analysis throughout much of the 20th century, building a rigorous theoretical framework for understanding markets and economic decision-making. This approach, while powerful, is based on a series of assumptions designed to simplify reality, enabling the development of predictive and normative models.

Basic Assumptions of Traditional Finance

Below, we explore the key principles that have guided this perspective.

1. Economic Agents are Rational

A fundamental pillar of traditional finance is the assumption that individuals make rational decisions, maximizing utility and minimizing costs. This assumption implies that:

- Investors process all available information logically.
- They select alternatives that offer the best balance between risk and return.
- Emotions or biases do not influence their decisions.

2. Markets are Efficient

The Efficient Market Hypothesis (EMH), proposed by Eugene Fama, posits that asset prices reflect all available information at any given time. In an efficient market:

- It is impossible to consistently achieve above-average risk-adjusted returns, as any new information is immediately incorporated into prices.

- Price anomalies are quickly corrected by market participants.

3. Financial Assets are Objectively Valued

Models such as the Capital Asset Pricing Model (CAPM) are based on the idea that assets have an intrinsic value determined by their systematic risk and expected return. This approach allows for the calculation of:

- The risk premium an investor requires for taking on uncertainty.
- The cost of capital, which is fundamental to corporate decision-making.

4. Diversification Minimizes Risk

Traditional finance emphasizes the importance of diversification as a strategy to reduce unsystematic risk. According to this perspective:

- Investors should build diversified portfolios to shield themselves from asset-specific fluctuations.
- The only risk relevant to expected returns is systematic risk, as it cannot be eliminated through diversification.

5. Information is Perfect and Free

This framework assumes that all market participants have access to the same information, which is truthful, complete, and immediately available. Additionally:

- There are no significant transaction costs that interfere with decision-making.
- Competition ensures that no participant has a sustained informational advantage.

6. Markets Operate Without Frictions

Another key assumption is the absence of market frictions, which implies that:

- Taxes, transaction costs, or regulatory constraints do not alter decisions.
- Bid and ask prices are identical.

A. Limitations of These Assumptions

While these principles have enabled the development of elegant mathematical models and practical tools, such as calculating the cost of capital, they reveal clear limitations when confronted with reality:

- Individual decisions are not always rational; they are influenced by emotions and biases.
- Markets are not always efficient; speculative bubbles and financial crises are examples of inefficiencies.
- Information is not always perfect or accessible to all participants.

These limitations have given rise to new approaches, such as behavioral finance, which seek to integrate the complexities of human behavior into financial analysis. However, understanding the foundations of traditional finance remains crucial, as they represent the starting point for building more modern models and theories.

B. Concrete Historical Examples

Success Case: CAPM in Investment Evaluation

In the 1970s and 1980s, the CAPM (Capital Asset Pricing Model) was widely used by companies and fund managers to evaluate investment projects and allocate resources. For instance, companies like General Electric adopted this model to determine the cost of capital for new divisions, calculating a risk premium aligned with specific sectors. This approach enabled strategic decision-making based on the relationship between risk and return, maximizing the efficiency of invested capital.

CAPM Limitation Case: Speculative Bubbles and the 2008 Financial Crisis

The 2008 crisis serves as a clear example of how markets can fail to reflect all available information. Before the collapse, the prices of mortgage-backed securities (MBS) failed to adequately account for the risk of widespread defaults. This failure contradicts the Efficient Market Hypothesis, demonstrating that prices can be influenced by irrational behavior, overconfidence, and misinformation.

C. Connection with Technological Development

Technology has transformed many of the basic assumptions of traditional finance:

- **More Accessible Information**: Tools like Bloomberg Terminal and Yahoo Finance provide real-time information to any investor, reducing informational asymmetry.
- **Challenges from Data Overload**: Although information is more accessible, investors face the challenge of separating relevant information from "noise." This contradicts the assumption of logical and rational processing of all available data.

A contemporary example is the use of artificial intelligence in trading platforms, where algorithms outperform humans in processing large volumes of data. However, they are not immune to failures due to emerging patterns or unprogrammed decisions.

D. Comparisons with Other Paradigms

Aspect	Traditional Finance	Behavioral Finance
Agent Decisions	Rational, utility-maximizing	Influenced by biases and emotions

Aspect	Traditional Finance	Behavioral Finance
Information	Perfect and free	Limited and processed with biases
Markets	Efficient	Affected by heuristics and panics
Risk	Quantifiable using mathematical models	Subjective, influenced by perceptions

E. Emerging Theories Evolving Traditional Assumptions

While CAPM and the Efficient Market Hypothesis (EMH) are cornerstones of traditional finance, new approaches aim to address their limitations:

- **Arbitrage Pricing Theory (APT)**: Proposed by Stephen Ross, this model incorporates multiple economic factors in asset valuation, overcoming the CAPM's exclusive reliance on systematic risk.

- **Behavioral Asset Pricing Model (BAPM)**: This approach integrates psychological and behavioral aspects into asset valuation, providing better explanations for market deviations during crises or periods of euphoria.

F. Practical Impact and Derived Tools

Traditional finance has given rise to widely used tools, including:

- **Markowitz Model**: The foundation of modern portfolio theory, formalizing the concept of efficient diversification.

- **Black-Scholes Model**: Crucial for the valuation of financial options, laying the groundwork for modern derivatives markets.

While these tools are essential, they have been adapted to account for limitations that arise in contexts of high volatility or irrational behavior.

G. Critical Reflection

To conclude, some final questions connect us to the chapters ahead:

- Are the assumptions of traditional finance still valid in a world dominated by big data and artificial intelligence?
- What challenges does human behavior, full of biases and emotions, pose to models that assume rationality?
- If markets are not entirely efficient, how can we improve predictive models to account for uncertainty and anomalies?

In the upcoming sections, we will explore these themes in greater depth.

The Efficient Market Hypothesis

The **Efficient Market Theory (EMT)** has been one of the cornerstones of modern finance, providing a framework for understanding how asset prices are formed in financial markets. Formulated primarily by Eugene Fama in the 1970s, this theory posits that asset prices reflect all available information in the market, implying that it is practically impossible for investors to achieve consistently superior returns without taking on additional risks.

EMT is based on three fundamental premises:

1. **Investor Rationality**: It is assumed that market participants process information logically and rationally, making decisions that maximize their utility.
2. **Availability of Information**: All relevant information, both public and private, is quickly incorporated into asset prices. This includes financial reports, corporate announcements, and external economic factors.

3. **Market Competition**: In a competitive market, agents are constantly seeking to exploit any price discrepancies, which quickly corrects any temporary inefficiencies.

Eugene Fama identified three levels of market efficiency, depending on the amount of information reflected in prices:

1. **Weak Form**:

Prices reflect all past information, including historical price and volume patterns.

This implies that profits cannot be made through technical analysis.

2. **Semi-Strong Form**:

Prices reflect all publicly available information, such as news, financial reports, and corporate announcements.

Fundamental analysis cannot generate extraordinary returns under this form.

3. **Strong Form**:

Prices incorporate all information, including private or insider information.

Under this level, even insiders cannot achieve sustained profits.

Implications of EMT

If markets are truly efficient:

Average Returns: Investors cannot consistently outperform the market's average risk-adjusted returns.

Passive Strategies: Passive investment strategies, such as replicating market indices, are promoted instead of attempting to outperform the market.

Accurate Valuations: Asset prices are a precise reflection of their intrinsic value.

Criticisms and Limitations

Despite its influence, EMT has faced significant criticism:

- ✓ **Existence of Anomalies**: Events such as the January effect, the value-size effect, and market overreactions challenge the idea of total efficiency.
- ✓ **Investor Irrationality**: Cognitive and emotional biases can lead to suboptimal decisions and the formation of speculative bubbles.
- ✓ **Information Processing**: The speed at which information is incorporated into prices is not always uniform, especially in less developed markets.

Relevance in the Current Context

The EMT remains a fundamental tool for understanding how markets operate, but its absolute nature has been nuanced by more recent approaches, such as behavioral finance. While markets may be efficient under normal conditions, in times of stress or uncertainty, biases, emotions, and cognitive limitations tend to take precedence.

Classical Models: CAPM and the Rational Expectations Hypothesis

In Traditional Finance, mathematical models and economic theories have played a central role in explaining asset prices and decision-making under conditions of uncertainty. Two of the most influential pillars of this approach are the Capital Asset Pricing Model (CAPM) and the Rational Expectations Hypothesis. These models have been fundamental to developing modern economic theory and financial practices.

Developed by William Sharpe, John Lintner, and Jan Mossin in the 1960s, the CAPM provides a simplified way to estimate an asset's expected return based on its risk relative to the market.

Assumptions of the CAPM:

1. **Efficient Markets:** Prices reflect all available information.
2. **Perfect Diversification:** Investors hold perfectly diversified portfolios that eliminate specific risk.
3. **Linear Risk-Return Relationship:** An asset's expected return depends solely on its systematic risk, measured by beta (β).
4. **Single Time Horizon:** All investors share the same time horizon.

Limitations of the CAPM:

- ✓ Markets are not always efficient, contrary to traditional finance assumptions.
- ✓ The model ignores additional factors that can influence prices, such as behavioral biases or macroeconomic events.
- ✓ The linear relationship between risk and return has been challenged by more advanced models, such as Fama and French's three-factor model.

The Rational Expectations Hypothesis

The rational expectations hypothesis, developed by John Muth and popularized by economists like Robert Lucas, argues that economic agents use all available information to form expectations consistent with the underlying economic models.

Fundamental Principles:

1. **Optimal Use of Information:** Individuals do not make systematic errors when forecasting the future.

2. **Coherence with the Model:** Expectations align with the predictions of the economic model that describes reality.
3. **Immediate Incorporation of New Information:** Agents quickly adjust their decisions in response to changes in market conditions.

Applications in Finance:

- **Asset Valuation:** Asset prices reflect the rational expectations of market participants about the future.
- **Economic Policy:** The actions of governments and central banks are already internalized in expectations, limiting the impact of anticipated interventions.

Criticisms of the Hypothesis:

- Economic agents do not always process information rationally due to cognitive and emotional biases.
- Rational expectations ignore the possibility of radical uncertainty, where the future cannot be predicted or modeled.
- In practice, individuals face costs and information limitations that make it difficult to form perfect expectations.

Relevance in the Current Context:

Both the CAPM and the rational expectations hypothesis have marked milestones in traditional finance, providing useful tools for decision-making. However, their ideal assumptions have been questioned by more recent research, including behavioral finance. Today, combining these classical models with more flexible approaches allows for a better understanding of the complexity of financial markets and decision-making in a dynamic and changing world.

Market Anomalies

Despite the elegance and simplicity of traditional theories, such as market efficiency and the CAPM model, reality has shown that financial markets do not always behave as predicted by these models. These deviations, known as market anomalies, challenge the fundamental principles of traditional finance and have been a primary motivation for the development of behavioral finance.

What Are Market Anomalies?

In the simplest terms, market anomalies are patterns or behaviors in asset prices that contradict the predictions of traditional models. These irregularities are difficult to explain under the assumption of investor rationality and market efficiency. Anomalies not only represent theoretical challenges but also offer practical opportunities for those seeking to capitalize on these patterns in their investment strategies.

Main Types of Anomalies

1. Calendar Anomalies

These anomalies reflect repetitive behaviors during specific days, months, or periods of the year.

- **January Effect**: Stock prices tend to rise more in January than in other months, especially for small-cap companies.
- **Day-of-the-Week Effect**: Lower returns on Mondays and higher returns on Fridays.
- **Year-End Effect**: Increases in stock prices due to year-end accounting strategies or holiday optimism.

2. Valuation Anomalies

These anomalies are related to how investors value assets, challenging the CAPM.

- **Size Effect**: Small-cap stocks often outperform large-cap stocks, contradicting the proportionality of risk and return.
- **Value Effect**: Stocks with low multiples (such as price-to-book or price-to-earnings ratios) tend to deliver higher returns than high-multiple stocks.

3. Technical Anomalies

- **Mean Reversion**: Assets with extremely high or low returns in one period tend to move back toward the mean in future periods.
- **Momentum**: Assets with strong recent performance tend to keep rising, while those with poor performance tend to continue falling, at least in the short term.

Possible Explanations from Behavioral Finance

1. Cognitive and Emotional Biases

Investors do not always process information rationally. For instance, overconfidence may lead to overvaluing certain assets, while fear can trigger panic selling.

2. Overreactions and Underreactions

- **Overreactions** occur when investors place too much weight on recent events, causing extreme price movements.
- **Underreactions** happen when markets are slow to incorporate new information, creating opportunities for momentum-based strategies.

3. Arbitrage Limitations

Although anomalies should disappear due to arbitrage activity, costs and risks in practice hinder this process, allowing anomalies to persist.

Impact on Investment Strategies

Market anomalies represent both risks and opportunities. While some investors attempt to exploit them through active strategies, others see them as signals to improve traditional models by incorporating behavioral aspects. These anomalies highlight the importance of understanding not only economic fundamentals but also the psychological and social factors that influence market behavior.

Criticism of Anomalies

Over time, the idea of market anomalies has been the subject of significant debate. While many consider them clear evidence of the failure of traditional models, others question their existence or real importance. Here are some of the most relevant criticisms:

1. The Uncaptured Risk Perspective

Critics argue that anomalies are not truly "anomalies" but rather compensation for unobserved or poorly modeled risks in traditional theories.

- **Example: Size Effect**

    Small-cap stocks may offer higher returns because they are riskier and less liquid, not because of a failure in the CAPM model.

- **Counterpoint**: Proponents of behavioral finance point out that the magnitude of these returns exceeds what would be expected from a simple risk adjustment.

2. Questionable Persistence

Some anomalies tend to disappear or become less significant once they are discovered and widely documented:

- **January Effect**: In recent years, it has declined in developed markets, possibly due to exploitation by investors and algorithms.
- **Counterargument**: This does not invalidate anomalies; it simply shows that markets adapt, as suggested by the adaptive markets hypothesis.

3. Data Bias Issues

- Many studies on anomalies rely on backtesting, which may introduce selection bias.
- Critics suggest that some anomalies are statistical artifacts: patterns that emerge in historical data but lack future relevance.
    - **Example**: Identifying a "Monday effect" could be a coincidence within a limited dataset.

4. Methodological Limitations

- Some economists believe that anomalies result from models that oversimplify reality. For instance, the CAPM assumes a single risk factor (beta), whereas markets are complex and multidimensional.
- **Recent Response**: Models like Fama and French's three-factor model and Carhart's four-factor model have attempted to address these limitations.

Incorporating Anomalies into Hybrid Models

To overcome the limitations of both traditional models and behavioral explanations, economists and analysts have developed hybrid approaches that combine elements from both worlds.

A. Multifactor Models

Multifactor models expand the CAPM framework by incorporating additional factors that better explain returns and capture some anomalies:

- **Fama and French Model**:

    Includes size and value as additional factors alongside beta.

    - **Captures**: The size effect and the value effect.
    - **Limitation**: Does not fully explain momentum.

- **Carhart Model**:

    Introduces the momentum factor, considering the tendency of assets to maintain their recent performance.

B. Machine Learning-Based Models

Technological advancements have enabled the development of models that dynamically identify and exploit anomalies:

- **Deep Neural Networks**:

    Use vast amounts of historical data to uncover nonlinear patterns that may correspond to complex anomalies.

Example: An AI model could identify micro-anomalies specific to an emerging market that shift with macroeconomic conditions.

- **Hybrid Systems**:

    Combine traditional data (prices, multiples) with unconventional inputs (social media sentiment, Google search data).

C. Adaptive Models

The adaptive markets hypothesis (Andrew Lo) posits that anomalies arise and fade depending on the evolution of economic agents:

- **Implication**: Anomalies are not permanent but adaptive.
- **Application**: Hybrid models based on this theory aim to capture these fluctuations in real-time.

D. Incorporation of Behavioral Aspects

- **Models Integrating Biases**:

    For instance, algorithms that include overconfidence or risk aversion as explanatory variables for market behavior.

E. Practical Applications

- **Portfolio Management**:

    Strategies that combine traditional principles (beta-based diversification) with opportunistic tactics based on momentum or mean reversion.

- **Crypto Markets**:

    Hybrid models have proven useful in capturing anomalies specific to the crypto market, such as movements driven by social media sentiment.

Conclusion

Hybrid models represent a significant advancement by integrating the best of traditional and behavioral finance. While market anomalies remain a theoretical challenge, their study and modeling drive innovation in investment tools and risk management. In an increasingly complex and technology-driven financial world, the ability to adapt to new anomalies will be key to staying competitive.

Challenges to the Rational Behavior Hypothesis

For much of the 20th century, traditional finance was built on the solid foundation of economic rationality. This concept, inherited from classical economic theory, assumes that economic agents act to maximize their utility, process information logically, and make optimal decisions in any context. While elegant and mathematically robust, this approach soon revealed cracks when confronted with the unpredictable and complex realities of financial markets.

In recent decades, the assumption of rationality has come under scrutiny, not only due to empirical anomalies observed in the markets but also because of growing evidence from psychology, neuroscience, and experimental economics. The collapse of the rational behavior hypothesis marks a turning point in how we understand finance, demanding a more human and interdisciplinary perspective.

The Appeal of Rationality: An Idealized but Limited Model

Rationality has been the conceptual core of models like the Efficient Market Hypothesis (EMH), proposed by Eugene Fama, and the Capital Asset Pricing Model (CAPM). According to these approaches, investors:

1. Have perfect and complete access to information and process it without error.
2. Evaluate risks and returns logically, maximizing their expected utility.
3. Act independently, free from external or emotional influences that might distort their decisions.

This theoretical framework enabled the development of widely used analytical tools and financial strategies. However, as the theory was applied to real markets, inconsistencies emerged that challenged its universal validity.

In a truly rational world, phenomena such as speculative bubbles, financial panics, and cycles of exuberance and irrationality should not exist. Yet history is replete with episodes where emotion, fear, and greed overpowered logic.

The Anomalies that Eroded Rationality

1. **Unexplainable Market Volatility**

   One of the earliest challenges to the rational paradigm came from Robert Shiller, who demonstrated that financial asset prices fluctuate far more than changes in their fundamental values would justify. This phenomenon, known as excessive volatility, directly contradicts the EMH and suggests that investors do not always react logically to available information.

2. **Bubbles and Financial Crashes**

   Events such as the 17th-century tulip mania, the 1929 crash, the dot-com bubble burst in 2000, and the 2008 subprime mortgage crisis are paradigmatic examples. These episodes reveal herd behavior, where individuals blindly follow market trends, often influenced by emotions like fear or euphoria. Individual rationality cannot explain these self-destructive dynamics.

3. **Findings from Experimental Economics**

   Experiments such as the ultimatum game and the dictator game show that people do not always act to maximize their economic benefit. In the former, many participants reject unfair offers, even if it means losing money, highlighting that values like fairness and reciprocity are as relevant as material benefit.

4. **Predictable Market Behaviors**

   Anomalies such as the January effect, the size effect, and price momentum challenge the idea of efficient and rational markets. They show that investors fall into predictable patterns and that prices do not always reflect all available information.

The Role of Psychology: Bounded Rationality

Economist Herbert Simon introduced the concept of bounded rationality, acknowledging that humans face cognitive and emotional constraints when making decisions. These limitations include:

- **Lack of complete information**: Investors may not have access to all relevant data or may be unable to process it adequately.
- **Reliance on heuristics**: Mental shortcuts, while useful, often lead to systematic errors or cognitive biases.
- **Influence of emotions**: Fear and greed are not anomalies but structural elements of how we make financial decisions.

Emotional Factors: The Human Side of Finance

Emotions are not accessories to rationality; they are an essential component of human behavior. Neuroeconomics has shown that financial decisions activate areas of the brain linked to emotional processing, such as the amygdala and the limbic system. Examples include:

- During a market downturn, fear may lead to panic selling, even when logic suggests holding the investment.
- Greed during bull markets can inflate speculative bubbles, disconnecting asset prices entirely from their fundamental value.

The Emergence of a New Paradigm

The collapse of the rationality hypothesis does not imply that traditional models are entirely invalid, but they must be complemented by more realistic and human-centric approaches. This paradigm shift has led to:

1. The expansion of behavioral finance, which integrates psychology, neuroscience, and economics to better understand market behavior.
2. The design of strategies that recognize and leverage investors' cognitive biases.
3. The questioning of traditional metrics, fostering new tools to value assets and assess risks.

The Resilience of the Rational Hypothesis in Certain Contexts

Although the rational behavior hypothesis has been widely questioned, its utility cannot be entirely dismissed. There are specific contexts where the assumptions of rationality remain valid or, at the very least, serve as useful theoretical and practical approximations. These contexts include:

1. **Highly Efficient Markets**

In financial markets dominated by institutional investors, such as sovereign bonds in developed countries or major stock indices, prices tend to adjust more quickly to available information.

- ✓ **Access to reliable and extensive information:** Participants in these markets are often well-informed and equipped with resources to analyze data more objectively.
- ✓ **Prevalence of quantitative algorithms:** The participation of algorithmic models in efficient markets reduces the influence of human emotions, reinforcing rational dynamics.
- ✓ **Practical example:** The U.S. Treasury bond market exhibits a closer correlation between prices and economic fundamentals compared to more volatile markets like cryptocurrencies or emerging-market equities.

2. **Strategic Decision-Making in Corporations**

In the corporate sphere, long-term investment and financing decisions are often grounded in rational assumptions:

- ✓ **Cost-benefit analyses:** Companies use tools like discounted cash flow (DCF) analysis to maximize shareholder value.
- ✓ **Risk management:** Hedging strategies employ financial derivatives based on traditional quantitative models.
- ✓ **Practical example:** A company deciding to build a new plant based on 10-year demand projections applies a rational approach by considering costs, expected returns, and associated risks.

3. **Quantitative Models as Approximations**

Although traditional models assume perfect rationality, many have proven useful as analytical tools, even when their assumptions are not fully met:

- ✓ **Simplified CAPM:** While investors are not perfectly rational, the Capital Asset Pricing Model (CAPM) remains a guide for calculating the cost of capital in corporate decision-making.
- ✓ **Diversified portfolios:** Modern Portfolio Theory (MPT) provides a framework for risk diversification, even when investors do not optimally maximize utility.

In summary, the rationality hypothesis remains a valuable reference point in certain environments where conditions approximate its assumptions. This suggests that its collapse is not absolute but relative to specific contexts.

Interdisciplinary Explanations for the Failures of the Rational Hypothesis

The questioning of the rational behavior hypothesis stems not only from empirical observations in markets but also from advances in disciplines such as neuroscience, evolutionary biology, and sociology, which provide new perspectives on human behavior:

1. Neuroscience: The Biological Basis of Irrationality

Neuroscience has revealed that financial decisions are influenced by emotional and automatic brain processes:

- **Loss aversion:** Activity in the amygdala during risky scenarios suggests that fear of loss is a stronger driver than the desire for gain, as described by Kahneman and Tversky's Prospect Theory.
- **Response to uncertainty:** In highly volatile situations, the limbic system can take control, reducing logical analysis capacity.
- **Practical example:** During abrupt market downturns, many investors panic-sell, even when logic would dictate holding positions.

2. Evolutionary Biology: Inherited Patterns

Seemingly irrational behaviors in markets may have evolutionary roots:

- **Herd behavior:** Following the group increased survival chances historically, but in financial markets, it can lead to speculative bubbles or crashes.
- **Preference for immediacy:** The tendency to prioritize short-term rewards over future benefits is linked to the historical struggle for scarce resources.
- **Practical example:** The cryptocurrency bubble illustrates how investors often follow trends driven by the fear of missing out.

3. Sociology: The Power of Group Norms

Sociology highlights how financial behaviors are not merely individual but also social:

- **Cultural norms:** A society's valuation of risk and reward influences collective financial decisions.

- **Group influence:** Dynamics within small groups or social media communities can amplify emotions like fear or euphoria, creating unexpected market movements.
- **Practical example:** Events driven by Reddit users, such as the GameStop case in 2021, show how communities can challenge traditional market dynamics.

4. Experimental Economics: Challenging Assumptions

Laboratory experiments have demonstrated that human decisions rarely align with economic rationality:

- **Results from the Ultimatum Game:** People reject unfair offers, even if it means losing money, revealing that values like fairness and reciprocity are as important as utility.
- **Difficulty in optimization:** When faced with multiple complex options, humans simplify decisions using heuristics, often leading to suboptimal outcomes.

Conclusion: A More Interdisciplinary Future

The collapse of perfect rationality marks a turning point but also an opportunity. By incorporating the human dimension into financial analysis, we are building a more comprehensive and robust framework. This new paradigm is not just about understanding numbers and charts but about understanding the people behind the decisions.

The future of finance will emerge from this interdisciplinary convergence, where psychology, economics, and artificial intelligence work together to explain and anticipate increasingly complex and dynamic human behavior.

PART II: THE BIRTH OF BEHAVIORAL FINANCE

Psychology Meets Finance

The collapse of the pure rationality model did not leave a theoretical void; instead, it opened the door to a broader and richer perspective: the integration of psychology with finance. In this context, it became evident that economic decisions are not solely the result of mathematical calculations but are also shaped by emotions, intuitions, and inherent cognitive biases. This interdisciplinary convergence gave rise to behavioral finance, a field that has transformed our understanding of markets and investors alike.

The Pioneers: Kahneman, Tversky, and Thaler

The development of behavioral finance would not have been possible without the foundational contributions of three key figures: Daniel Kahneman, Amos Tversky, and Richard Thaler.

1. Daniel Kahneman and Amos Tversky: The Psychological Roots of Financial Decisions

Kahneman and Tversky, both trained psychologists, revolutionized the understanding of decision-making under uncertainty. Their experiments revealed that humans are not always rational and that their choices are deeply influenced by cognitive biases.

Their most influential contribution is the **Prospect Theory**, a groundbreaking alternative to traditional models of expected utility. This theory demonstrates that individuals evaluate gains and losses asymmetrically, experiencing greater sensitivity to losses than to equivalent gains.

2. Richard Thaler: Bridging Psychology and Economics

Thaler applied these psychological insights to economics and finance, showing how cognitive and emotional biases influence decisions related to investment, saving, and consumption. His concept of **mental accounting** explains how people irrationally categorize their money, assigning different emotional values to equivalent funds depending on the context.

Thaler also popularized the idea of **nudges**—small changes in choice architecture that influence behavior without restricting freedom of choice. These principles have found applications in public policy and investment strategies alike.

Decisions Under Uncertainty: Prospect Theory

Proposed by Kahneman and Tversky in 1979, **Prospect Theory** is a cornerstone of behavioral finance. This model challenges rationality assumptions by revealing that people:

1. **Perceive gains and losses relatively, not absolutely.** For example, gaining $100 feels more satisfying to someone expecting $50 than to someone expecting $200.
2. **Exhibit risk aversion in gain scenarios** but take greater risks to avoid losses. This explains why investors often hold on to losing assets, hoping to recover their value, rather than cutting losses.
3. **Suffer from anchoring effects,** where decisions are influenced by arbitrary reference points, such as the original purchase price of a stock.

The theory also introduced the concept of the **value function**, showing how individuals evaluate potential outcomes:

- The **gain curve** is concave, indicating diminishing satisfaction with additional increments.

- The **loss curve** is convex and steeper, reflecting that losses are psychologically more intense than gains.

This model not only reshaped economic theory but also provided a framework for understanding everyday market phenomena, such as speculative bubbles and excessive risk aversion.

Cognitive and Emotional Biases

A lasting legacy of Kahneman, Tversky, and Thaler is their identification of cognitive and emotional biases that distort decision-making. Below are some of the most relevant:

Cognitive Biases

1. **Overconfidence:**
   Investors often overestimate their own abilities and underestimate risks, leading to excessive trading or ignoring warning signals.

2. **Confirmation Bias:**
   People seek information that supports their pre-existing beliefs, disregarding evidence that contradicts them. This can amplify bullish or bearish trends, fueling bubbles or panics.

3. **Anchoring:**
   As noted in Prospect Theory, investors frequently rely on arbitrary reference points, such as past prices, to guide current decisions.

4. **Availability Bias:**
   This occurs when people overvalue recent or easily recalled events, ignoring statistically significant data.

Emotional Biases

1. **Loss Aversion:**

The psychological pain of loss is so intense that it leads to irrational decisions, such as panic-selling or holding onto unprofitable assets.

2. **Ambiguity Aversion:**

   Investors prefer options with clearer outcomes, even when those options are objectively less favorable.

3. **Herding Effect:**

   Also known as "herding behavior," this bias drives individuals to follow popular trends without critical analysis.

4. **Fear and Greed:**

   These primal emotions drive extreme market behavior, fueling both speculative bubbles and financial collapses.

Examples of Cognitive and Emotional Biases in Finance

Cognitive Biases

1. **Overconfidence**

Example: A novice investor makes profits on their first stock trades and begins to believe they have a natural talent for investing. Without thorough analysis, they allocate most of their portfolio to high-risk tech stocks, confident their decisions will always succeed. When the market corrects and stocks plummet, they suffer significant losses.

2. **Confirmation Bias**

Example: An investor is convinced the energy sector will rebound. Instead of considering negative reports about declining oil demand, they focus solely on optimistic articles and forecasts that reinforce their belief. This leads them to invest in oil companies just before crude prices fall further.

3. **Anchoring**

Example: An investor buys a stock at $100 per share. Even though the company's fundamentals deteriorate and the stock price drops to $60, they refuse to sell, clinging to the idea that the price must return to $100. This behavior ties them to an irrelevant benchmark rather than reevaluating the investment using current data.

4. **Availability Bias**

Example: A friend tells an investor how they made a fortune investing in Bitcoin. This anecdote strongly influences the investor, who then decides to invest heavily in cryptocurrencies without researching their volatility or risks, relying solely on their friend's personal experience.

Emotional Biases

1. **Loss Aversion**

Example: An investor buys shares that lose 20% of their value. Although they know the company is facing serious issues, they refuse to sell to avoid realizing the loss. This reluctance worsens their outcomes when the stock continues to decline.

2. **Ambiguity Aversion**

Example: Two investment options are available: a) A bond with a guaranteed 3% return; b) A stock fund with an expected 7% return but some uncertainty.

Despite the stock fund's higher expected return, the investor chooses the bond, fearing the risks associated with uncertainty.

3. **Herd Behavior (Herding)**

Example: During a housing bubble, an investor notices many people are buying properties. Despite suspecting that prices are overinflated, they purchase an apartment, thinking, "Everyone is making money; I can't miss out." The bubble bursts, and the investment's value plummets.

    4. **Fear and Greed**

Example:

Greed: An investor sees a stock rise 20% in a few days. Ignoring the company's fundamentals, they buy in, hoping the stock will continue rising. However, the market corrects, and they lose money due to inadequate evaluation.

Fear: During a market downturn, another investor panics and sells all their stocks at low prices, despite not needing immediate liquidity. When the market recovers, they miss out on potential gains.

R. Shiller, Irrational Exuberance, and Narratives

Robert Shiller's work is a cornerstone of behavioral finance. As a Nobel laureate in 2013, he challenged the traditional view of markets as efficient and rational systems by exploring how psychological and social factors shape asset prices. His seminal contributions include the book *Irrational Exuberance* and his focus on the power of economic narratives.

Irrational Exuberance

In *Irrational Exuberance* (2000), Shiller examines how speculative bubbles arise from emotional behavior and collective psychology rather than solid economic fundamentals. Using the late 1990s tech bubble as an example, he demonstrated how markets overvalue assets when driven by euphoria and greed, rather than rational analysis.

A notable example is the mid-2000s housing bubble, which Shiller predicted before its collapse in 2008. His Case-Shiller Index, measuring

U.S. home prices, highlighted the unsustainable growth in real estate values. This phenomenon was fueled by the widespread belief that "housing prices never fall," a powerful narrative that led millions to overextend financially.

Shiller argues that irrational exuberance is not merely the result of individual choices but a collective psychology that amplifies emotions like fear and greed, ultimately causing severe market imbalances.

The Power of Economic Narratives

In *Narrative Economics* (2019), Shiller introduced a groundbreaking perspective, asserting that stories and narratives, rather than cold data, drive economic decisions. These narratives spread like viruses, shaping expectations and behaviors in individuals and markets.

Example Narratives: A) The notion of "Bitcoin as digital gold" has attracted millions of investors, often unaware of its volatility or technological underpinnings. B) The idea of "The Chinese Miracle" has spurred massive investment in Asian emerging markets, even when these economies face structural risks.

Shiller emphasizes that economic narratives are crucial for understanding phenomena like bubbles, financial crises, and even long-term trends. Unlike traditional theories focused on numbers and data, his approach highlights the significant impact of human emotions and shared stories on market behavior.

Intersection of Exuberance and Narratives

What distinguishes Shiller's work is his ability to link irrational exuberance with the power of narratives. Bubbles don't form in isolation; they require compelling stories to capture investors' attention. Narratives like "technology will revolutionize the world" can inflate the valuations of tech companies far beyond reasonable levels, as seen during the dot-com bubble.

Shiller's legacy not only challenges traditional finance but also offers a more human and realistic perspective on how markets operate. His concepts of irrational exuberance and economic narratives are vital tools for any investor or analyst seeking to understand markets beyond mere numbers.

New Generations of Researchers: An Evolving Legacy

The foundational work of Kahneman, Tversky, and Thaler has given rise to an interdisciplinary movement that continues to evolve. New generations of researchers have delved deeper into cognitive biases and extended the scope of behavioral finance into cultural, technological, and social contexts.

1. **Cultural Diversity and Regional Biases**

Researchers like Shlomo Benartzi and Hersh Shefrin have explored how cultural differences shape risk perception and financial decisions. For instance, collectivist societies are generally more risk-averse than individualist ones, affecting their investment, saving, and consumption behaviors.

2. **Behavioral Economics and Generational Shifts**

Millennials and Gen Z exhibit unique financial behaviors, prioritizing sustainability and transparency in investments. This has driven the rise of ESG (Environmental, Social, and Governance) strategies, integrating ethical values into portfolio management.

3. **Big Data and Artificial Intelligence Applications**

Advanced technologies are transforming investor behavior analysis. Scholars like Andrew Lo have integrated behavioral insights with quantitative methods, creating hybrid models that combine psychology, AI, and big data to predict market behavior. These innovations have led to automated systems that mitigate human biases in real time, enhancing investment decisions.

4. Biases in Extreme Contexts

Recent studies have examined how biases manifest in high-uncertainty scenarios, such as economic crises or global disruptions (pandemics, geopolitical conflicts). Researchers like Nicholas Barberis have shown how fear and risk aversion intensify in these contexts, triggering herd behavior and financial panics.

5. Applied Neuroscience

Neuroeconomics combines behavioral finance with biology and neuroscience, uncovering how the brain processes economic decisions. Recent discoveries highlight the roles of the amygdala and prefrontal cortex in risk aversion and impulsive decisions. These advances pave the way for behavioral therapies and more personalized strategies to manage biases.

COROLLARY: A NEW WAY TO VIEW MARKETS

The integration of psychology into finance has unveiled that markets are not merely an aggregation of rational decisions but a reflection of human complexities. Every stock trade, every investment choice, is imbued with a web of emotions, biases, and cognitive limitations.

Thanks to the pioneers of behavioral finance, we now understand that markets are both psychological and economic. In this duality lies not only their complexity but also immense potential for those who learn to navigate their human dynamics.

Neuroscience Meets Finance

At the intersection of neuroscience and finance, a revolutionary discipline has emerged: neurofinance. This field employs techniques such as functional magnetic resonance imaging (fMRI) to observe how the human brain reacts to investment decisions and financial risks.

Santiago Ramón y Cajal, the great Spanish neurologist and Nobel Prize winner in Medicine (1906), described neurons as "butterflies of the soul," whose flutter could reveal the secrets of mental life. Today, these "butterflies" help us understand not only the workings of the brain in health but also how emotions, neurotransmitters, and neural processes influence the chaotic dynamics of financial markets. In markets, emotions are not mere passengers—they are the drivers.

Reason and Emotion: Two Sides of the Same Coin

The traditional belief that financial decisions are purely rational has been debunked by multiple studies. As neuroscientist Antonio Damasio stated: "We do not think and then exist; we exist, and then we think." Emotions guide reason, not oppose it. This is particularly evident in investing, where emotional markers influence every decision, from the best to the worst ones.

For instance, an investor buying stocks hopes for an immediate price increase, but if prices drop, their brain enters an emotional paralysis, irrationally expecting losses to reverse. This behavior reflects one of the most common biases: loss aversion. These emotional dynamics are fundamental to understanding phenomena like financial bubbles and abrupt crashes.

The Role of Somatic Markers

Neuroscience has shown that financial decisions rely not only on present information but also on past experiences. The concept of "somatic markers" explains how we associate certain options with pleasant or unpleasant emotions. These markers act as shortcuts, speeding up decision-making, especially in high-pressure environments like financial markets. However, this speed comes at a cost: precision is sacrificed, increasing the likelihood of errors.

Additional Neuroscience Topics

In volatile and risky environments, even the most experienced investors make mistakes. This occurs because our brains, evolved over millions of years to solve basic survival problems, are not perfectly adapted to the complexities of modern financial markets.

Traditional economics assumes that the mistakes of some investors are offset by the rationality of others, creating balance. However, in practice, emotional biases are often shared by large groups, leading to herd behavior. Thus, investors are not irrational due to a lack of calculations but because their decisions are deeply influenced by emotional reactions.

Money as a Reward

Another groundbreaking finding in neurofinance is that money activates the same brain reward circuits as food, drugs, or even attractive faces. This suggests that money has not only instrumental value but also intrinsic value, providing pleasure even when not spent. This phenomenon might explain why we spend so much time and energy accumulating wealth and why we experience pain when parting with it.

The Brain as a Predictive Machine

Recent discoveries reveal that the human brain does not merely react to external stimuli but operates as a predictive machine. During a market downturn, for instance, the brain not only interprets the event but also compares it with past experiences, adjusting its response. However, these predictions are dominated by the limbic system, responsible for emotions, often leading to overestimations of risk or overreactions to losses.

From the Invisible Hand to Animal Spirits

While Adam Smith explained capitalism's stability through his famous "invisible hand," Keynes introduced the concept of "animal spirits," referring to the emotional impulses underlying economic instability. Neurofinance seeks to reconcile these approaches, exploring how stability and chaos can arise from the human nervous system.

The Power of Dopamine in Decision-Making

One of the most fascinating findings in neurofinance is the role of dopamine, a key neurotransmitter in the brain's reward system. When investors gain profits, their brains release dopamine, creating a pleasurable sensation that encourages repetitive behavior. However, this mechanism can be dangerous, as excessive dopamine release may lead to overconfidence and disproportionate risk-taking, as seen in financial bubbles.

For example, during the late-1990s dot-com bubble, many investors became addicted to the thrill of winning, ignoring clear signs of overvaluation. By analyzing these dynamics, neurofinance helps us understand how the brain can become either an ally or an adversary in financial decision-making.

The Role of the Amygdala in Financial Crises

The amygdala, a small brain structure responsible for processing emotions like fear, plays a crucial role during periods of high volatility. During a financial crisis, the amygdala can dominate decisions, triggering irrational responses such as panic selling or decision paralysis. This phenomenon, known as emotional hijacking, explains why markets tend to fall faster than they rise: fear is a much more potent and urgent emotion than euphoria.

Algorithmic trading systems, designed to eliminate the human factor, aim to mitigate these responses, though they do not entirely escape the biases of their programmers.

The Evolution of Neurofinance: From the Laboratory to the Real Market

Initially, neurofinance relied on controlled experiments, such as analyzing how participants responded to simple financial choices. However, technological advancements have enabled this research to extend into real-world scenarios. Today, tools like eye-tracking and heart rate sensors are used to study traders' behavior in real time.

In a famous experiment, traders with greater variability in their heart rates adapted better to high-uncertainty environments because they were more attuned to their emotions. Findings like these are now being applied to design emotional training programs for investors, improving their ability to withstand financial stress.

Conclusion: Neurofinance as a Learning Tool

Neurofinance sheds light on the emotional and neurological foundations of our financial mistakes, but correcting them requires time and adaptation. This trial-and-error process is inherent to the human brain, which continues to adjust to a world of complex financial decisions. Meanwhile, neuroscience findings advance our understanding of markets, providing tools that could transform how we invest and manage risk.

Case Studies: When Behavior Changed Markets

Human behavior has proven to have a decisive impact on financial markets, shaping bubbles, crises, and boom-and-bust phenomena. Through the following case studies, we can observe how biases, emotions, and narratives drove irrational movements that challenged traditional financial principles.

The Dot-Com Bubble

The dot-com bubble is a quintessential example of how rampant speculation and behavioral biases can inflate markets to unsustainable levels. This event not only marked the rise and fall of late 20th-century tech companies but also provided key lessons for future market cycles.

The Boom: A Compelling Narrative

The 1990s were marked by optimism surrounding the transformative potential of the internet. Emerging tech companies, known as "dot-coms" due to their online presence, promised to revolutionize entire industries. This narrative captivated retail and institutional investors, who believed that any internet-related company was destined for success.

The markets were inundated with IPOs of tech startups, many of which lacked solid revenues or sustainable business models. At the bubble's peak, valuations soared to levels disconnected from any reasonable metric, fueled by optimistic projections and a steady flow of capital.

Behavioral Factors in the Boom:

- **Overconfidence and optimism:** Investors believed the exponential growth of the internet would guarantee success for all tech companies, underestimating associated risks.

- **Collective euphoria:** Enthusiasm for dot-coms created a "fear of missing out" (FOMO), prompting even skeptics to enter the market to avoid missing apparent gains.

- **Confirmation bias:** Investors sought information to validate their beliefs about the inevitable success of dot-coms, ignoring warning signs like weak balance sheets and consistent losses.

The Collapse: A Reality Check

By 2000, the euphoria began to unravel as financial results failed to meet inflated expectations. Investors, realizing many business models were unviable, began selling shares en masse.

The NASDAQ index, home to most tech companies, plunged from a peak of over 5,000 points in March 2000 to under 1,200 by October 2002. Iconic companies like Pets.com, Webvan, and Boo.com went bankrupt, while others barely survived.

Enduring Lessons:

1. **The importance of fundamentals:** The bubble underscored that valuations must ultimately be backed by solid business models and revenue generation.

2. **The dangers of herd behavior:** Herding and social influence can lead to massive market overvaluation, emphasizing the need for informed and independent decision-making.

3. **Innovation vs. risk:** While technology opens new opportunities, not all innovative companies are guaranteed success. Distinguishing visionary ideas from viable business models is critical.

4. **The role of regulation and media:** Regulators and financial media played mixed roles. Poor oversight and excessive promotion of IPOs fueled the bubble, highlighting the need for transparency and financial education.

5. **Resilience and opportunity:** Despite the bubble's destruction of wealth, it paved the way for the technological resurgence of companies like Amazon, eBay, and Google, which learned from the bubble's mistakes and built sustainable long-term businesses.

Conclusion

The dot-com bubble is a vivid reminder of how markets can be driven by psychology as much as fundamentals. Though painful, this crisis provided lessons that continue to guide investors and regulators in understanding market cycles.

The Subprime Crisis

The 2008 financial crisis, triggered by the collapse of the U.S. subprime mortgage market, is a stark example of how the interplay between human psychology and financial markets can have catastrophic consequences. This event transformed the global economy, destabilized the financial system, and offered critical lessons on the importance of regulation and risk management.

The Boom: An Illusion of Stability

In the years leading up to the crisis, the U.S. housing market experienced an unprecedented boom, driven by low interest rates, easy access to credit, and the widespread belief that "housing prices always rise." This narrative encouraged the proliferation of subprime loans, granted to borrowers with poor credit histories and high default risk.

Banks, seeking to maximize profits, bundled these loans into complex financial instruments like collateralized debt obligations (CDOs) and sold them to investors worldwide, relying on deceptively high credit ratings from rating agencies.

Behavioral Factors at Play:

1. **Overconfidence:**

Financial institutions assumed risks were dispersed and managed through securitization, underestimating systemic collapse correlations.

Rating agencies exhibited overconfidence in financial models supporting AAA ratings for subprime products.

2. **Confirmation bias:**

Investors and regulators ignored warning signals, focusing on data supporting the booming housing market narrative.

Borrowers also succumbed to this bias, convinced they could refinance their mortgages indefinitely as property values rose.

3. **Loss aversion:**

Homeowners clung to the hope of recovery, refusing to sell during price drops, exacerbating market inventory issues.

Banks delayed acknowledging losses on their balance sheets, prolonging market uncertainty.

The Collapse

The system began unraveling in 2007 as subprime mortgage defaults surged. Housing prices, which had reached record highs, started falling sharply, eroding the value of mortgage-backed securities.

The impact was amplified by the interconnectedness of financial markets:

- Structured products tied to subprime mortgages lost value rapidly, leaving banks and funds with toxic assets.
- A lack of trust in counterparties led to a credit crunch, halting the flow of money between financial institutions.
- Lehman Brothers, a major Wall Street firm, collapsed in September 2008, marking a turning point in the crisis.

Key Lessons from the Subprime Crisis:

1. **The danger of collective narratives:**

    The crisis demonstrated how shared beliefs can inflate bubbles and create a false sense of security.

2. **Transparency in financial markets:**

   The opacity of structured financial instruments magnified risks. A lack of understanding about their mechanics prevented proper risk assessment.

3. **The role of regulation:**

   Financial deregulation, combined with reckless lending practices, facilitated systemic risk accumulation. The crisis underscored the need for robust oversight and strict financial product standards.

4. **Behavioral biases and their impact:**

   Biases like overconfidence, loss aversion, and confirmation bias affected not only individual investors but also institutions and regulators, highlighting the importance of incorporating behavioral finance into risk management.

5. **The interconnectedness of the global financial system:**

   The crisis revealed how interdependent economies and financial markets are, demonstrating that issues in one sector or country can trigger global crises.

Conclusion

The subprime crisis was more than a financial collapse; it was a reflection of human vulnerabilities mirrored in markets. Understanding the psychological and structural factors behind this event is crucial for avoiding similar mistakes in the future.

The 2008 financial crisis was one of the most devastating events in modern history, triggered by excessive confidence in the U.S. housing market. The dominant narrative, "house prices never fall," led to the proliferation of subprime loans (high-risk mortgages) and the creation of complex financial products based on these loans.

- **The Role of Behavior:**

Overconfidence: Banks assumed risks were adequately dispersed through securitizations.

Confirmation bias: Investors ignored warning signs, focusing on data that supported their belief in an ever-expanding housing market.

Loss aversion: Many homeowners refused to sell as prices began to fall, worsening the crisis.

- **The Collapse:**

When housing prices fell, subprime borrowers began defaulting, and the financial instruments tied to these mortgages quickly lost value. This triggered a global credit crisis and the collapse of iconic institutions like Lehman Brothers.

- **Lessons Learned:**

The subprime crisis highlighted how shared beliefs can create bubbles and how a lack of transparency in financial products can amplify risks. It also underscored the importance of proper market regulation.

The Volatility of Cryptocurrencies

The cryptocurrency market, led by Bitcoin, has experienced multiple boom-and-bust cycles fueled by both technological innovation and speculative behavior. The prevailing narratives of cryptocurrencies as "the future of money" and "a decentralized store of value" attracted millions of investors worldwide.

- **The Role of Behavior:**

FOMO (Fear of Missing Out): Many investors bought cryptocurrencies simply because others were profiting, without understanding the risks.

Overconfidence: Crypto enthusiasts underestimated market volatility, assuming prices could only rise.

Compelling Narratives: Concepts like Bitcoin as "digital gold" and Ethereum as "the new internet" captivated investors' imaginations.

- **Booms and Busts:**

2017: Bitcoin peaked at nearly $20,000 but quickly dropped below $4,000 in 2018, reflecting an initial bubble burst.

2021-2022: A new bull run driven by institutional interest and mass adoption pushed Bitcoin above $60,000, followed by a crash below $20,000 after collapses like Terra/Luna and FTX.

2023-2024: Following the turbulent 2022, efforts to rebuild trust in cryptocurrencies emerged. Bitcoin showed signs of recovery, stabilizing at higher ranges and regaining institutional investor interest, reigniting the bubble vs. fundamentals debate.

- **Regulation at the Forefront:**

In 2023-2024, global governments advanced clearer regulatory frameworks. The U.S., European Union, and emerging economies focused on consumer protection, transparency, and anti-money laundering measures.

- **Technological Adoption and Real-World Applications:**

Cryptocurrencies found practical use cases in international payments, remittances, and inflation-prone economies. Blockchain projects like scalability solutions (Layer 2) and smart contracts demonstrated utility beyond speculation.

- **New Market Narratives:**

The market adopted more diverse narratives, with growing interest in decentralized finance (DeFi), non-fungible tokens (NFTs), and stablecoins backed by traditional currencies as more stable alternatives in a volatile ecosystem.

- **Impact of Artificial Intelligence:**

AI integration with blockchain technology became an emerging trend. AI-driven data and predictions played a role in analyzing and managing crypto portfolios, paving the way for new investment strategies based on behavior and predictive analytics.

- **Persistent Risks:**

Despite advancements, the 2023-2024 period faced persistent challenges:

Market volatility driven by macroeconomic decisions, such as interest rate hikes.

Failures of smaller cryptocurrencies due to liquidity issues and lack of adoption.

Security breaches, such as decentralized platform hacks, reinforcing the need for more robust solutions.

Overall, the past years have been a transitional period, marked by a search for balance between innovation, regulation, and trust restoration. While challenges remain, the foundation established during this time promises a more mature and resilient future for the cryptocurrency ecosystem.

- **Behavioral Lessons:**

The cryptocurrency market highlights how narratives, behavioral biases, and regulatory gaps can drive extreme volatility. It also emphasizes the importance of a cautious approach in emerging and innovative markets.

Other Major Historical Bubbles

Tulipomania: The Netherlands, 1636-1637

Imagine that a single tulip cost as much as a luxury home. During Tulipomania, tulip bulbs reached exorbitant prices driven by speculative fever. As prices rose, more people joined in buying, thinking they could sell at even higher prices. This classic example of herd behavior shows how the fear of missing out led many to ignore the true value of the asset. When the bubble finally burst, prices plummeted, and many investors lost everything.

The South Sea Bubble: England, 1720

The South Sea Company promised high returns to its investors, triggering massive euphoria. The expectation of profits caused the price of its shares to skyrocket to unsustainable levels. Here, the halo effect played a significant role, as investors viewed the company with exaggerated optimism and overlooked warning signs of risk. In the end, when the business turned out to be far less profitable than promised, prices collapsed.

The Railway Bubble: U.S. and Europe, 1840s-1850s

With the rise of railways, a wave of enthusiasm emerged to invest in this technology that promised to revolutionize transportation. However, excessive optimism and low-risk perception led to overinvestment. Here we see the classic loss aversion bias, where investors preferred to "bet" on seemingly safe railway projects, ignoring the risks of overvaluation. When expectations weren't met, losses were inevitable.

The Crash of 1929: U.S.

The 1920s was a period of euphoria in the U.S. stock market, where many believed that stock prices would just keep rising. However, behavioral economics shows that behind this belief was cognitive dissonance: investors ignored risk signs and justified their investments because they wanted to take advantage of "easy gains." This irrational behavior contributed to the crisis that triggered the Great Depression, a time when prices collapsed and dragged millions of people into ruin.

COROLLARY

The cases analyzed make it clear that financial markets are not simply a sum of rational transactions based on objective data. On the contrary, they are deeply influenced by human emotions, collective narratives, and cognitive biases that shape investors' decisions. The dot-com bubble, the subprime crisis, and cryptocurrency market cycles remind us that, in finance, behavior matters as much as fundamentals.

These events also highlight the importance of an interdisciplinary approach to financial analysis. Understanding the psychology behind investment decisions and how narratives spread can help anticipate trends and prevent crises. However, this is not only relevant for academics or analysts: individual investors, regulators, and businesses also have much to gain by adopting a more behavioral perspective.

The study of anomalies and irrational behavior in markets is not just an academic exercise. It is a practical tool to build more stable, transparent, and resilient markets. In an increasingly interconnected world prone to volatility, understanding how and why collective decisions deviate from rationality can make the difference between financial success and failure.

Finally, these cases prepare us to explore how behavioral finance not only explains the past but also offers tools to navigate the future. The next challenge will be to integrate these concepts with new technologies, such as artificial intelligence, to develop systems that not only understand human behavior but also anticipate and manage it in real-time. This approach will be key to facing the financial challenges of the 21st century.

PART III: THE PRESENT OF BEHAVIORAL FINANCE

Current Tools and Applications

The progress in behavioral finance is not limited to explanatory theories but has also led to practical tools and innovative applications that are transforming how investors and managers interact with financial markets. Among these tools, the concept of *Behavioral Alpha* and the design of nudges in financial markets stand out.

Behavioral Alpha: How Managers Leverage Behavior

The term *Behavioral Alpha* refers to the ability of asset managers to generate returns above the market average by exploiting behavioral biases and irrational patterns in financial markets. Unlike traditional alpha, which relies on analytical skills to identify undervalued assets, Behavioral Alpha capitalizes on inefficiencies caused by investor behavior.

Managers implementing Behavioral Alpha might, for example, observe overreaction behaviors in bearish markets where certain asset prices drop excessively due to widespread panic. By acquiring these undervalued assets and selling them once prices stabilize, they gain returns from the market's correction.

A. Common Strategies to Capture Behavioral Alpha:

1. **Informed Contrarianism:** Buying when others are selling out of fear and selling when market euphoria dominates.

2. **Adapted Momentum:** Identifying trends in their early stages and strategically positioning before the broader market follows suit.

3. **Managing Client Irrationality:** Financial advisors can use knowledge of clients' emotional biases to guide them toward more rational decisions, avoiding common mistakes like panic selling.

Behavioral Alpha particularly thrives during periods of high volatility or economic uncertainty when behavioral biases tend to intensify. This highlights the importance of understanding emotions and the psychology of market participants as a competitive advantage.

B. Specific Biases Facilitating Behavioral Alpha

Behavioral Alpha leverages systematic investor errors driven by their behavioral biases. These biases not only affect individual participants but also ripple into amplified market movements:

- **Anchoring Effect:** Investors often anchor their decisions to an initial reference point, like previous prices or outdated forecasts, even when updated information contradicts them. This can lead to temporary undervaluations or overvaluations of assets.

- **Loss Aversion:** This strong bias explains why many investors prefer to avoid losses, even at the expense of forgoing potential gains. It's particularly evident in bearish markets, where emotional pressure outweighs rationality.

- **Disposition Effect:** Many investors hold on to losing assets, hoping they will "recover" their initial value, ignoring indicators suggesting otherwise. This behavior creates opportunities for those who can identify fundamentally solid assets.

Example: During a market correction, managers may identify assets trading below intrinsic value due to widespread panic, gaining returns by buying when others are selling.

C. Differences Between Behavioral Alpha and Traditional Alpha

Behavioral Alpha differs from traditional alpha in several key aspects:

- While traditional alpha focuses on fundamental and quantitative analysis, Behavioral Alpha exploits human emotions and irrational behavior. This requires a blend of technical skills and knowledge of crowd psychology.
- Another critical difference lies in the timeframe. Traditional alpha may take years to materialize, while Behavioral Alpha is often captured over shorter periods, particularly during volatile episodes.

Example: Traditional managers seek undervalued companies based on solid financial projections. In contrast, managers pursuing Behavioral Alpha observe collective behavioral patterns, like impulsive selling after negative news, to act contrary to the consensus.

Practical Example: A client may receive real-time alerts when attempting impulsive buy or sell decisions, or a firm may optimize financial products designed to prevent common investor mistakes, such as buying high and selling low.

D. Technological Tools for Detecting Behavioral Biases

With technological advancements, managers have increasingly sophisticated tools to identify and leverage behavioral patterns, particularly for Behavioral Alpha:

- **Data Mining:** Analyzes vast amounts of data from social media, financial forums, and news to detect early signals of collective emotions. For example, a spike in "fear" keywords on Twitter could signal an upcoming bearish market.
- **Sentiment Analysis:** Using Natural Language Processing (NLP) algorithms, texts are evaluated for emotional tone. Managers

can use these analyses to anticipate market moves driven by emotions.

- **Machine Learning:** Predictive models process historical and real-time data to identify correlations and human behavior patterns that traditional methods might miss.

These tools allow managers to interpret the "emotional pulse" of the market with greater precision and speed than ever before.

E. Behavioral Alpha in Emerging Markets

Emerging markets provide ideal conditions for capturing Behavioral Alpha:

- **Lower Transparency and Regulation:** Incomplete or asymmetric information amplifies behavioral biases. Investors react more to rumors or partial news, creating opportunities for informed managers.
- **High Volatility:** Frequent economic and political fluctuations create fertile ground for panic and euphoria—two emotions that distort prices.

Example: During a period of political uncertainty in Argentina, local investors may overreact to headlines, leading to a mass sell-off of stocks. An experienced manager could capitalize on this irrationality by purchasing quality assets at discounted prices.

F. Ethical Considerations in Using Behavioral Alpha

Behavioral Alpha poses an ethical dilemma: Is it morally acceptable to profit from others' irrationality? While managers argue that they are merely correcting market inefficiencies, critics suggest these practices may perpetuate inequalities in financial knowledge access.

Additionally, there's a risk of incentivizing speculative practices or manipulating less-experienced investors' behavior. A potential ethical solution might involve balancing alpha generation with financial education, helping investors recognize and mitigate their own biases.

G. Limitations and Risks of Behavioral Alpha

Despite its advantages, Behavioral Alpha is not infallible:

- **Uncertainty in Patterns:** Behavioral biases do not always manifest predictably. External events, such as natural disasters or regulatory changes, can disrupt typical behavior patterns.
- **Over-Optimization Risk:** Models based on historical data may become overly specific, failing when market conditions change.
- **Overconfidence:** Managers relying too heavily on Behavioral Alpha may underestimate fundamental factors, compromising their strategies.

Example: A manager may purchase assets assuming a market overreaction, only to discover that prices reflected genuine structural changes in a company's fundamentals.

H. Evolution of Behavioral Alpha in Active Management

The concept of Behavioral Alpha has evolved from an academic idea to a strategy implemented by advanced investment funds:

- In the 1990s, behavioral finance began challenging the efficient market hypothesis, demonstrating that human biases could create persistent inefficiencies.
- Today, Behavioral Alpha is integrated into hybrid models combining behavioral analysis with advanced quantitative methods, maximizing the potential of both disciplines.

I. Real-Life Case Studies

One relevant case involves funds specializing in contrarian strategies, such as Warren Buffett's approach. Although Buffett does not explicitly focus on behavioral finance, his philosophy of "being greedy when others are fearful" exemplifies Behavioral Alpha principles.

Another modern example includes funds using sentiment analysis to invest in cryptocurrencies—a highly emotional and volatile market.

J. Behavioral Alpha and Alternative Investment Vehicles

Beyond stocks and bonds, Behavioral Alpha can be captured in:

- **Derivatives:** Managers identify distorted option prices caused by irrational market expectations.
- **Cryptocurrencies:** The impulsive and emotional behavior of participants creates opportunities for behavioral arbitrage.
- **Art Markets or Illiquid Assets:** Lack of standardized information amplifies the influence of biases, creating opportunities for informed managers.

K. Financial Education to Counter Biases

Financial education plays a critical role in both protecting investors from their errors and reducing opportunities for exploitation:

- **Recognizing Biases:** Teaching investors about herd behavior, loss aversion, and other common biases can help them make more rational decisions.
- **Using Tools:** Technology-based advisory applications can counter emotions in decision-making.

Ultimately, a market with more informed investors is more efficient and stable, benefiting all participants.

Designing Nudges in Financial Markets

Nudges are interventions designed to influence people's decision-making without limiting their freedom of choice. Introduced by Richard Thaler and Cass Sunstein, nudges have become a powerful tool in financial markets, helping investors avoid costly mistakes and promote more optimal decisions.

A. Examples of Nudges:

- **Automatic Retirement Savings:** Many financial companies set pension contributions as opt-out rather than opt-in. This means that employees are automatically enrolled unless they choose otherwise, which significantly increases savings rates.

- **Use of Default Options in Investment Portfolios:** Investment platforms often propose default portfolios designed to match the client's risk profile. This helps prevent investors, especially beginners, from selecting inappropriate options.

- **Education Based on Visual Feedback:** Tools that show interactive graphs of how small regular investments can grow over time motivate investors to be more disciplined.

- **Reorganization of Options:** In trading platforms, placing less risky options in more prominent positions can help investors avoid speculative investments without proper understanding.

B. Impact of these Tools on the Market

These tools reflect a significant shift toward a more inclusive and efficient market, where financial institutions not only compete for profits but also seek to guide their clients toward healthier financial behavior. The use of Behavioral Alpha allows managers to identify hidden opportunities and exploit market psychology, while nudges empower investors to make more conscious decisions. Both trends highlight how the combination of finance and behavioral sciences not only explains the past but also shapes the future of the financial sector.

C. Types of Nudges in Financial Markets

Nudges in financial markets can be classified into different categories based on their approach:

- **Informational:** Present financial data clearly and understandably, helping users make informed decisions. For example, a simple graph comparing the long-term cost of different loan options can influence the choice of a less costly financial product.
- **Structural:** Rearrange financial processes to facilitate desired behaviors. For example, setting up savings plans as an opt-out option allows more people to participate without the need for additional effort.
- **Emotional:** Appeal to feelings like security or fear to influence decisions. An example would be highlighting how a retirement plan can ensure financial peace of mind in old age.

D. Digital Nudges in Fintech Platforms

Fintech platforms have revolutionized the implementation of nudges by combining intuitive design and real-time data analysis:

- **Push Notifications:** Automatic reminders about bill due dates or minimum payments to avoid penalties.
- **Personalized Suggestions:** Based on spending habits, apps can recommend adjustments, such as reducing entertainment expenses to meet savings goals.
- **Gamification:** Incorporating gaming dynamics in financial tools, such as showing progress bars toward savings goals, motivates users to maintain disciplined behavior.

E. Ethical Nudge Design

While nudges are powerful tools, their design raises ethical dilemmas. An ethical approach ensures that nudges benefit the user:

- **Transparency:** Informing the client about how the nudge is structured and its possible consequences.
- **Avoid Manipulation:** Designing nudges that do not exploit cognitive biases for the exclusive benefit of the financial institution, such as prioritizing products that are more profitable for the bank but less favorable for the user.

A controversial case can arise when an app suggests financial products with hidden fees or inferior benefits.

F. Nudges for Institutional Investors

Nudges are not exclusive to individual investors; they can also influence the decision-making of fund managers and institutional investors:

- **Data Reorganization:** Presenting the risks associated with certain investments prominently, such as the impact of geopolitical events on diversified portfolios.
- **Exposure Alerts:** Using algorithms to identify when a portfolio has too much concentration in a specific sector or asset and recommending diversification. For example, a nudge might warn about risks arising from excessive exposure to technology companies in a context of rising interest rates.

G. Impact of Culture and Context on Nudges

Nudges must adapt to the values, culture, and level of financial development of the market:

- **Emerging Markets:** In these contexts, where financial education is limited, nudges can simplify basic decisions like saving for

emergencies or using insurance. For example, SMS campaigns reminding users to deposit small amounts regularly.
- **Developed Markets:** In advanced economies, nudges can address more complex decisions, such as tax optimization, portfolio diversification, and estate planning.

H. Measuring the Effectiveness of Nudges

Evaluating the impact of nudges is essential to adjust their design:

- **Quantitative Indicators:** Changes in the percentage of users who save regularly, a decrease in the use of costly financial products, such as high-interest credit cards.
- **Qualitative Indicators:** Improvement in users' financial understanding, detected through surveys before and after implementing a nudge.

For example, a 20% increase in the savings rate among users of a financial app would indicate the success of the nudge.

I. Success Stories of Financial Nudges

- **Savings in Nordic Countries:** Automatic savings systems in countries like Sweden have increased participation rates in pension plans, achieving greater financial security for citizens.
- **Microfinance in India:** Several institutions have implemented SMS reminders that improve repayment rates in group loans, reducing delinquency.

These cases demonstrate how small nudges can have a large impact on financial behavior.

J. Nudges in Sustainable Investment Strategies (ESG)

Nudges can promote responsible investments aligned with environmental, social, and governance (ESG) criteria:

- **Highlighting Positive Impacts:** Showing investors how their choices contribute to sustainable development.
- **Default Portfolios:** Offering ESG portfolios as a default option, promoting a shift toward more ethical investments. In this context, tools that visualize the carbon footprint associated with a portfolio can influence the investor's decision.

K. The Future of Nudges with Artificial Intelligence

AI promises to personalize nudges to unprecedented levels:

- **Real-Time Analysis:** Detecting spending or investment patterns and recommending immediate adjustments.
- **Educational Chatbots:** Providing clear explanations about financial products, dispelling doubts before making decisions. For example, a chatbot could warn about risks associated with a personal loan with variable rates in inflationary contexts.

L. Nudges in Financial Regulation

Regulators can also employ nudges to protect consumers:

- **Clear Standards:** Requiring financial institutions to present product comparisons with total long-term costs.
- **Mandatory Warnings:** Including visible messages on complex products, such as warnings about leverage in investments. This can foster a safer and more accessible financial environment.

Nudges represent a unique convergence of psychology, economics, and technology, offering a powerful tool to improve financial decision-making. By subtly but effectively influencing behavior, these interventions have the potential to democratize access to financial products, optimize investment strategies, and promote more responsible practices at both the individual and institutional levels.

However, the success of nudges does not solely depend on their technical design but also on ethics and transparency in their application. When used responsibly, they can transform financial markets into more inclusive, sustainable spaces aligned with the interests of participants. As technologies like artificial intelligence and machine learning advance, nudges will become even more personalized and effective, solidifying their role as one of the most promising tools at the intersection of behavioral sciences and finance.

The future challenge lies in balancing their increasing sophistication with the need to protect users from potential manipulation, ensuring these "small pushes" are always a driver of financial well-being and not a mechanism for exploitation. With the proper implementation, nudges will not only change investor behavior but also reshape the global financial landscape.

The Role of Technology in Behavioral Finance

Technology has revolutionized every aspect of finance, and behavioral finance is no exception. Tools such as Big Data, predictive models with artificial intelligence, and investor sentiment indices have taken the ability to analyze and predict behavior in financial markets to unprecedented levels. This transformation has allowed managers, analysts, and investors to anticipate market movements with increasing accuracy by leveraging the wealth of data and the power of modern algorithms.

Big Data and Behavioral Analysis

Big Data has enabled the collection, storage, and analysis of massive amounts of information about financial markets and investor behavior. Every transaction, online search, social media post, and news headline generates data that can be analyzed to better understand the decisions of market participants.

Applications in Behavioral Finance:

1. **Detection of Behavioral Patterns:** Algorithms can identify trends in real-time, such as sudden increases in searches for keywords related to economic crises or spikes in fear or euphoria posts on social media.

2. **Analysis of News and Social Media:** Natural Language Processing (NLP) enables the classification of the tone of news and messages on platforms like Twitter, providing signals about the prevailing sentiment in the market.

3. **Investor Segmentation:** Financial institutions can segment their clients based on their behavioral profile and offer personalized investment strategies.

Big Data not only reveals what is happening but also helps explain why investors behave in certain ways, based on external events, emotions, and global trends.

Special Topics in Financial Big Data

A. Predicting Investor Behavior Using AI

The use of advanced machine learning algorithms allows Big Data to be analyzed to predict investor reactions to specific events. For example, changes in interest rates, elections, or global crises generate search patterns, transactions, and changes in trading volume that AI can identify. These tools not only anticipate potential downturns or recoveries but also detect anomalies in behavior, such as unusual activity from institutional investors before key announcements.

These predictions not only benefit large financial institutions but are also starting to democratize through platforms accessible to retail investors. Tools like pre-trained models on historical trends or interactive dashboards allow users to assess probable market responses before making important decisions, thus reducing reliance on traditional experts.

B. Use of Biometrics and Personal Data in Financial Analysis

Advances in wearable devices and biometric sensors have opened the door to collecting emotional and physiological data in real time. Variables such as heart rate, cortisol levels, and brain activity can be correlated with risk decisions. For example, high stress has been shown to increase risk aversion, while euphoria leads to overbuying behaviors. Integrating this information with transaction data would allow financial institutions to better understand the emotional states that drive investor decisions.

Additionally, these technologies could be implemented in educational programs and financial simulation platforms. Beginner investors could visualize how their physiological reactions impact their trading choices, fostering deeper learning on emotional regulation and decision-making under pressure.

C. Impact of Cognitive Biases Detected in Large Data Volumes

Big Data helps identify common biases in investors, such as:

- **Overconfidence:** Investors tend to make more frequent transactions in bull markets, which can be detected through transaction frequency analysis.
- **Loss Aversion:** Analyzing how investors quickly sell winning assets while holding onto losing ones longer than expected.
- **Availability Bias:** Spikes in searches for negative news correlated with impulsive selling decisions are another example.

Fund managers can also leverage this knowledge to design anti-bias strategies. For instance, creating personalized alerts to inform investors about their repetitive behavioral patterns, encouraging more rational decisions. This also opens the possibility of generating financial products that include insurance against biased behaviors.

D. Interaction Between Big Data and Neuroeconomics

Neuroeconomics studies how areas of the brain respond to financial incentives. Big Data broadens this field by identifying how unconscious patterns, such as responses to digital advertising, influence investment decisions. For example, combining functional magnetic resonance imaging (fMRI) data with online search analysis can reveal how risk and reward preferences are formed.

Moreover, neuroeconomics based on Big Data could help redesign financial products, optimizing their appeal based on observed emotional responses. For example, the visual presentation of a product could be adapted to reduce stress associated with high-risk investments, increasing the likelihood of customer acceptance.

E. Dynamic Market Sentiment Models

Market sentiment indices have evolved thanks to Big Data. Nowadays, algorithms can analyze millions of social media posts, news headlines, and search volumes in real-time, creating more accurate and up-to-date metrics than the Fear & Greed Index. These dynamic indices allow fund managers to anticipate movements before traditional indicators show clear signals.

These tools are also being used to build proactive strategies rather than reactive ones. For example, some hedge funds implement models that automatically adjust their positions when market sentiment indices change rapidly, allowing them to seize opportunities or reduce risks in highly volatile markets.

F. Big Data in Emerging Markets

Emerging markets, such as those in South America and many others, present unique challenges such as limited access to reliable data and higher emotional volatility among investors. Big Data allows the capture of specific behaviors in these markets, such as trading patterns associated with local political events. Additionally, social media analysis in these countries shows how rumors and informal news affect financial decisions.

As more regional databases and analysis platforms are developed, Big Data can also help level the playing field between emerging and developed markets. This fosters broader integration into global markets, making data-driven decisions more reliable and less dependent on speculation.

G. Ethics and Privacy in Big Data Use

The use of personal data for financial strategies raises significant ethical dilemmas. Institutions must balance the benefit of offering personalized services with the protection of user privacy. For example, trading platforms that track social media data could create unfair advantages for certain investors, in addition to potential violations of data protection regulations like GDPR.

Technological advances have also led to new regulations, such as the use of transparent and auditable algorithms. These controls aim to ensure that Big Data analysis respects both privacy and fair market conditions, minimizing the risk of algorithmic discrimination.

H. Advanced Behavioral Data Visualization

Visualization tools, such as interactive dashboards and network graphs, make complex patterns more comprehensible. For example, a chart showing the relationship between "economic crisis" searches and market drops can offer retail investors a clear and accessible perspective, democratizing access to behavioral data.

The incorporation of visual narratives with augmented reality (AR) or virtual reality (VR) technologies could further revolutionize financial data analysis. This would allow investors to "explore" trends and relationships intuitively, helping them identify opportunities or risks more quickly.

I. Big Data and Mass Personalization

Big Data analysis allows financial institutions to develop large-scale personalized products. Algorithms can segment clients not only based on traditional demographic data but also by behavioral patterns, risk levels, and emotional preferences. This results in investment strategies that are more aligned with individual objectives, increasing customer satisfaction and retention.

Personalization also extends to dynamic portfolio design, which automatically adjusts asset composition based on changes in detected customer emotions through surveys or digital interactions, promoting a more proactive and satisfying relationship.

J. Integrating Social Media Analysis with Volatility Metrics

The correlation between social media activity and market volatility is an emerging area of study. For example, analysis of cryptocurrency-related posts has proven useful in predicting volatility spikes. Integrating this data with traditional metrics, such as the Volatility Index (VIX), can provide more robust signals for investors.

A deeper integration could also benefit regulatory institutions, allowing them to anticipate extreme speculative movements and take preventive measures. For example, certain algorithms could identify coordinated social media campaigns that artificially influence prices, thus protecting more vulnerable investors.

Conclusion

The impact of Big Data on financial behavioral analysis is transformative, enabling a deeper and more accurate understanding of investor decisions. From detecting patterns and biases to mass personalization and trend prediction, these tools are redefining how we interact with markets. However, this advancement also poses ethical and technical challenges that must be addressed rigorously to ensure a balance between innovation, fairness, and privacy. Ultimately, Big Data not only promises to improve market efficiency and transparency but also democratizes access to knowledge, allowing both institutions and individual investors to make more informed decisions aligned with their goals.

Predictive Models with Artificial Intelligence

Artificial Intelligence (AI) has taken behavioral data analysis to the next level. Thanks to its ability to learn complex patterns and make accurate predictions, AI models have become a key tool in investment management and market analysis.

Features and Advantages:

1. **Prediction of Bubbles and Corrections:** Machine learning models can identify early signs of irrational behavior, such as excessive optimism in specific sectors, anticipating corrections before they occur.

2. **Extreme Personalization:** AI algorithms can analyze an individual investor's decision history and suggest personalized strategies that reduce the impact of emotional biases.

3. **Dynamic Portfolio Optimization:** AI can automatically adjust investment portfolios based on market sentiment and real-time economic conditions.

Example: An AI-based investment fund could detect that an increase in searches related to "recession" coincides with a rise in U.S. Treasury bond sales. The fund could then adjust to prioritize safe-haven assets, anticipating the market movement.

Topics with Development Potential in Predictive Models

A. Explainability of Predictive Models (Explainable AI, XAI)

In finance, transparency in predictive models is critical, as investors and regulators need to understand how and why certain decisions are made. Explainable AI (XAI) aims to unravel the "black box" of algorithms, providing clear and justifiable interpretations. For example, a model recommending selling shares of a company might support its decision by showing a detailed analysis of the impact of a recent earnings drop, combined with sentiment analysis of negative social media posts and financial news.

The development of XAI tools not only boosts trust in AI but also facilitates the identification of errors or biases in the model, which is crucial to avoid decisions that could harm investors or the market in general.

B. Hybrid Models: AI and Traditional Approaches

Hybrid models combine AI's analytical power with traditional financial approaches such as technical or fundamental analysis. This integration allows predictive models to leverage both historical patterns and emotional market dynamics.

For example, a hybrid model could use fundamental analysis to assess a company's financial statements while simultaneously employing AI to analyze online search patterns reflecting a change in investor interest in the sector. This combination not only increases the accuracy of predictions but also provides a broader context that aids in strategic decision-making.

C. Incorporation of Alternative Data

AI has enabled the incorporation of unconventional data into predictive models, expanding the horizons of financial analysis. Examples of alternative data include satellite images to measure inventory in ports, weather data to predict agricultural yields, or traffic patterns to assess consumer flow to shopping malls.

When processed with advanced algorithms, this data can provide a significant competitive advantage. For example, a hedge fund could anticipate a drop in sales at a supermarket chain by observing a decrease in customer traffic in real time, even before quarterly results are released.

D. Impact of Generative AI on Predictive Models

Generative AI, such as ChatGPT and other language models, is revolutionizing predictive models by enabling more intuitive interactions with financial data. These tools can generate detailed reports, simulate future scenarios, and even suggest investment strategies in natural language.

For example, a financial advisor might ask a generative AI model, "What sectors are most likely to grow in the next six months based on current data?" and receive a comprehensive analysis, supported by charts and statistics. This not only improves the accessibility of predictions but also accelerates the decision-making process.

E. AI in Emerging and High-Volatility Markets

Emerging markets present unique challenges, such as a lack of structured data and volatile economic conditions. AI-based predictive models are particularly useful in these contexts, as they can process incomplete data, identify hidden trends, and quickly adapt to sudden changes.

For example, in a country where political fluctuations directly impact the market, an AI model could predict a decline in the value of the local currency by analyzing the negative tone of political speeches or mass protests reported on social media.

F. Bias in Financial AI Models

A major challenge for AI predictive models is the presence of biases in training data. If historical data reflects discriminatory patterns or incorrect decisions, the model could perpetuate those errors. For instance, a model that prioritizes investments solely based on large market capitalizations could overlook opportunities in emerging niche companies.

To mitigate these risks, developers are implementing "de-biasing" techniques, which adjust algorithms to neutralize biases and ensure a more balanced and fair analysis.

G. Predicting Geopolitical Risks

Geopolitical risks are one of the largest sources of uncertainty in financial markets. AI predictive models are designed to analyze vast amounts of data related to global events, such as conflicts, economic sanctions, or regulatory changes.

For example, a model could detect an increase in trade tensions between two countries by analyzing news headlines and social media mentions, suggesting that investors reduce exposure in vulnerable sectors such as technology or energy.

H. Applications of AI in Algorithmic Trading

AI is taking algorithmic trading to new levels of precision and speed. Algorithms can execute thousands of trades in milliseconds, analyzing micro-signals from the market, such as fluctuations in spreads or order volumes.

Moreover, AI allows strategies to be adjusted in real-time. For example, if a model detects a sudden decrease in the liquidity of an asset, it could automatically rebalance a portfolio to minimize potential losses, leveraging its ability to process multiple variables simultaneously.

I. Use of Deep Neural Networks (Deep Learning)

Deep neural networks are advanced tools that identify patterns in complex, nonlinear data, such as financial market behavior. These networks are especially useful in predicting asset prices, where relationships between variables are often highly dynamic.

For example, a neural network could analyze millions of historical and current data points, such as interest rates, implied volatility, and market sentiment, to predict the future price of an asset with great accuracy.

J. Ethics and Regulation of Predictive AI

As AI becomes a key player in finance, concerns about its ethical and regulatory impact arise. Issues such as data privacy, unfair use of information, and the possibility of market manipulation require a robust regulatory framework.

For example, regulators might require predictive models to include a full traceability of their decisions, ensuring they are not based on insider information or discriminatory practices.

Conclusion

Predictive models powered by artificial intelligence are revolutionizing financial analysis, providing tools that are more accurate, dynamic, and personalized than ever before. From identifying complex patterns to incorporating alternative data and adapting in real-time to volatile markets, these technologies are redefining how investment decisions and risk management are made.

However, this progress also comes with significant challenges, such as the need for greater transparency, bias mitigation, and the establishment of solid ethical and regulatory frameworks. As AI becomes more deeply integrated into finance, its true potential will depend on balancing innovation with responsibility, ensuring these tools not only optimize financial performance but also benefit all stakeholders in the ecosystem. In this new paradigm, artificial intelligence is not just a tool, but a strategic partner in building a more efficient and equitable financial future.

Investor Sentiment Index

An investor sentiment index measure the predominant emotions in the market, such as optimism, fear, or risk aversion, and have become essential tools for understanding and predicting collective behaviors.

Construction and Use:

- **Data Sources:** These indices rely on multiple sources, such as social media, financial news, investor surveys, and market data.
- **Methodology:** They use natural language processing (NLP) and machine learning algorithms to classify sentiments and generate an aggregated "optimism" or "pessimism" score.

Impact on Investment Decisions:

- ❖ **Prediction of Volatility:** An increase in fear sentiment generally precedes periods of high market volatility.
- ❖ **Identification of Opportunities:** Managers can take advantage of moments of panic to acquire undervalued assets or avoid sectors with excessive optimism that may be overvalued.
- ❖ **Risk Management:** Sentiment indices help adjust hedging strategies based on market emotions.

Trends in Investor Sentiment

- ❖ **Expansion of Data Sources**

Traditional sentiment indices often rely on surveys and financial news, but the growing volume of alternative data provides more sophisticated signals. Sources such as earnings call transcripts, comments on specialized forums (e.g., Reddit for meme stocks), and search patterns on engines like Google offer unique insights into investors' emotions. These sources help capture early signs of collective behavior before they are reflected in prices.

❖ **Real-Time Market Sensors**

High-frequency data, such as buy/sell order flows, bid-ask spreads, and implied volatility, adds a critical time dimension. Indices that integrate these sensors allow real-time reactions to sudden changes in sentiment, improving the accuracy of investment strategies.

Advanced Methods for Index Construction

❖ **Use of Deep Neural Networks**

While traditional algorithms like keyword-based sentiment analysis are effective, deep learning neural networks can interpret more complex contexts. For example, the term "crash" might be negative in a financial context but irrelevant in another. Deep Learning models remove these ambiguities, allowing for more accurate classification.

❖ **Custom Indices**

Segmenting sentiment indices by sectors (technology, energy, healthcare) or geographic regions is a promising innovation. This customization helps investors understand the emotions prevalent in specific areas of interest, offering more relevant signals for their individual strategies.

Integration with Other Financial Indicators

❖ **Relationship with Technical Indicators**

Combining sentiment indices with technical tools such as RSI, moving averages, and Bollinger Bands can improve the identification of market entry and exit points. For example, an extreme pessimism index combined with an oversold RSI may indicate a solid buying opportunity.

❖ Correlation with Macroeconomic Indices

Sentiment indices can act as leading indicators of key economic variables. For example, a sustained increase in pessimism could correlate with future economic slowdowns or recessions. This allows managers to adjust strategies before official numbers are released.

Historical Studies and Empirical Validation

❖ Behavior During Past Crises

Analyzing how sentiment indices behaved during events like the 2008 financial crisis, the collapse of Lehman Brothers, or the COVID-19 pandemic is essential for validating their usefulness. These analyses can show how abrupt changes in sentiment anticipated sharp market movements.

❖ Robustness Testing

In addition to historical analysis, testing the robustness of indices across different time horizons (short, medium, and long term) and under various market conditions, such as high or low volatility, is crucial. This helps determine in which contexts they are most reliable.

Specific Applications by Investor Profile

❖ Retail Investors

Sentiment indices can help small investors avoid common mistakes such as "panic selling" or "blind optimism." Mobile applications based on these indices could offer alerts or practical advice, such as "Avoid selling during this panic moment."

- **Institutional Managers**

For institutional investors, sentiment indices offer a competitive advantage by identifying trends before they become apparent. For example, they can adjust portfolios to protect against volatility caused by massive emotional shifts.

New Strategic Applications

- **Bubble Detection**

Sentiment indices can identify speculative bubbles by measuring extreme optimism disconnected from economic fundamentals. For example, during the tech bubble of the 2000s, such an index would have detected excessive euphoria in the sector.

- **Impact on Emerging Markets**

In emerging markets, where emotional decisions have a disproportionate impact due to lower liquidity and inherent volatility, sentiment indices can be a key tool. They allow managers to anticipate extreme movements and protect against additional risks.

Future Perspectives

- **Global vs. Regional Sentiment**: With the globalization of markets, distinguishing between local and global emotions becomes essential. For instance, an index that combines global and regional sentiment can help detect how international events, such as U.S. elections, affect local markets.
- **Generative AI in Sentiment**: Generative AI tools like ChatGPT could generate automatic sentiment summaries, explaining in simple terms which emotions dominate and what implications they have for the market, facilitating decision-making.

Ethics and Regulation

- **Sentiment Manipulation**

The existence of sentiment indices raises the risk of manipulation, where powerful actors in social media or media outlets could influence emotions for their own benefit. It is important to establish regulations that minimize these risks.

- ❖ **Data Privacy**

Ensuring the privacy of individuals whose social media interactions or internet searches are used to build indices is crucial for maintaining trust in these tools.

Advanced Visualization

- ❖ **Sentiment Heatmaps**

Graphical tools like heatmaps can show how sentiment varies across different sectors, regions, or even specific assets, making complex data easier to interpret.

- ❖ **Emotional Narratives**

Visualizations that show the temporal evolution of predominant emotions (e.g., spikes in fear or optimism during specific events) can help identify recurring patterns useful for future strategies.

In Summary

Investor sentiment indices today represent a powerful fusion between behavioral psychology and advanced technology, allowing financial markets to access an emotional dimension that complements traditional analysis. Their ability to detect trends, anticipate movements, and adjust strategies makes them indispensable tools for both individual and institutional investors. As data sources diversify and methodologies improve, these indices will not only help understand the past and present of the market but also illuminate the path towards more informed and resilient decision-making in the future. The integration with emerging technologies and an ethical approach to their development will ensure that they remain relevant and reliable in an increasingly complex financial environment.

Conclusion: Technology and Behavioral Finance, A Transformative Synergy

The impact of Big Data, artificial intelligence, and sentiment indices goes beyond traditional analysis. These tools are bridging the gap between traditional and behavioral finance, providing new levels of information on the emotions and decisions of investors. With an ever-growing capacity to understand and predict human behavior, technology not only amplifies the reach of behavioral finance but also redefines how we interact with global markets.

Cryptocurrencies and Blockchain: Hype or Real Transformation?

Cryptocurrencies have emerged as one of the most disruptive financial innovations of the last decade. Since the creation of Bitcoin in 2009, these blockchain-based digital currencies have sparked both fervor and skepticism. Advocates argue that cryptocurrencies represent the future of money, offering a more efficient, transparent, and decentralized financial system. On the other hand, critics view them as a speculative bubble reliant on mass psychology and expectations of high returns rather than stable intrinsic value.

In this context, behavioral finance plays a crucial role. Cryptocurrencies, like previous financial bubbles, appear to be heavily influenced by investor behavior. Buying and selling decisions are often motivated by greed, fear, and speculation, leading to extreme price volatility. Investors tend to overreact to available information, sometimes driven by rumors, sensationalist news, or the desire to "not miss out" on the next big opportunity. This creates cycles of euphoria and panic, hallmarks of financial bubbles.

The impact of cryptocurrencies extends beyond financial markets, also transforming the way we conceive money, transactions, and trust in institutions. The underlying blockchain technology, which enables transparent and secure transactions without intermediaries, has been recognized as an innovation with applications beyond cryptocurrencies, such as in smart contracts, digital voting, and supply chain management systems. However, despite their potential benefits, mass adoption faces obstacles, including regulatory issues, technological barriers, and public perception that cryptocurrencies are a volatile and risky investment.

The role of psychology in the cryptocurrency market is a promising phenomenon, highlighting how human emotions influence economic behavior. "FOMO" (fear of missing out) is one of the main drivers behind impulsive purchases, while panic over price drops can trigger mass sell-offs, exacerbating volatility. Additionally, the lack of clear intrinsic value, as with traditional assets, increases the influence of perceptions and expectations. This dynamic clearly reflects how principles of behavioral finance, such as overreaction to risk and availability biases, are deeply embedded in how investors approach the cryptocurrency market.

Tokenized Finance

The tokenization of assets is revolutionizing how investors access markets. Through tokenization, a tangible or intangible asset is converted into a digital token on the blockchain, allowing the fractionalization of traditionally illiquid assets such as real estate, art, or even business shares. This opens new possibilities for greater financial inclusion, enabling investors to access these markets with smaller amounts of capital.

However, as with cryptocurrencies, tokenized finance is not free from behavioral risks. The appeal of token investments may be influenced by the perception of participating in a cutting-edge trend, potentially leading to overvaluation of these assets. Investors might make decisions based more on collective euphoria than on solid fundamental analysis. Moreover, the decentralized nature of tokenization platforms could create a false sense of security and transparency, while the lack of regulation might facilitate speculative behaviors.

The tokenized finance market is constantly expanding, and its ability to democratize access to previously inaccessible assets holds transformative potential. For instance, in the case of real estate, tokenization allows small investors to purchase fractions of properties, which previously required substantial amounts of capital. This fractional access not only improves asset liquidity but also fosters diversification in investment portfolios. Similarly, the tokenization of artwork and tangible assets offers a new avenue for investment in markets traditionally exclusive to a limited number of participants.

Nevertheless, the emergence of these new forms of investment also poses challenges in terms of investor psychology. A lack of understanding of the underlying tokenization processes and associated risks can lead to hasty decisions and overconfidence in decentralized platforms. In an emerging market, speculation could be exacerbated by the sense of investing in something "innovative," prompting investors to take excessive risks without properly evaluating the actual value of the underlying assets. Moreover, the inherent volatility of decentralized markets can generate erratic fluctuations in token prices, potentially causing investors to overreact, falling into the same pitfalls of past financial bubbles.

Market Sentiment and Volatility

Market sentiment plays a crucial role in the volatility of cryptocurrencies and tokenized assets. As mentioned in earlier chapters, markets are not entirely rational, and investors' decisions are influenced by emotional and psychological factors. Collective sentiment can trigger sharp price movements in digital assets.

The extreme volatility of cryptocurrencies, in particular, can be attributed to a combination of behavioral biases such as the "bandwagon effect" (the tendency to follow the crowd) and "overconfidence." When sentiment is positive, investors tend to overvalue assets, driving prices to unsustainable levels. In moments of panic, such as Bitcoin's price drop in 2018 or the FTX collapse in 2022, investors overreact, engaging in mass sell-offs and exacerbating price declines.

Furthermore, cryptocurrency volatility is not solely caused by individual investors. Large market players, known as "whales," also play a significant role by moving substantial sums in single transactions, significantly affecting prices and fueling speculation.

The influence of market sentiment on volatility is not limited to retail investors' emotions but also involves macroeconomic factors and global events. Cryptocurrencies, for instance, are highly sensitive to news, rumors, and regulatory changes that can generate peaks of optimism or fear, amplifying price fluctuations. As investors react to these stimuli, collective psychology is reflected in market volatility, sometimes overriding economic fundamentals and leading to overvaluation or undervaluation of assets. The fear of "missing out" or "losing money" drives quick, emotional decisions, increasing the likelihood of unforeseen volatility.

Institutional actors and large entities (whales) also have a disproportionate effect on either stabilizing or exacerbating this volatility. Their capacity to move significant amounts of cryptocurrencies or tokenized assets rapidly can disrupt market equilibrium, forcing small investors to reactively adjust. When prices are driven by speculative trends, whale movements can cause sharp oscillations, fueling cycles of irrational optimism or mass panic. This behavior, driven by both collective sentiment and the actions of major players, highlights the vulnerability of digital markets to investors' emotions and psychology, potentially resulting in heightened volatility and the formation of speculative bubbles.

Behavioral Decisions in Decentralized Environments

Cryptocurrencies and blockchain have introduced a new paradigm: decentralized environments. These systems operate without the need for traditional intermediaries, such as banks or governments, offering users greater control over their assets. However, this also brings unique behavioral challenges.

One of the main challenges is the "illusion of control," which leads users to feel more secure and competent in decision-making when, in reality, the complexity of these systems can result in costly errors. In a decentralized environment where transactions are irreversible and assets are not backed by traditional entities, investors may fall into the trap of overestimating their ability to manage risks.

Additionally, in these decentralized environments, the lack of regulation can foster a "high-risk, high-reward" mentality, leading to impulsive and risky decisions. The absence of oversight can also intensify behavioral biases such as "loss aversion," where investors overreact to price drops, or "reciprocity," where users blindly follow others' recommendations without rigorous analysis.

In decentralized environments, the lack of intermediaries can also create a false sense of autonomy and confidence, leading investors to take unnecessary risks. Decentralization removes traditional control structures, such as financial regulations, leaving users more vulnerable to fraud or technical failures. This sense of freedom can induce overconfidence, where investors believe they are entirely in control of their decisions and assets, without accounting for the inherent risks of the digital environment. As blockchain technology and cryptocurrencies grow in popularity, this behavioral challenge of overestimating control can result in substantial losses for those who do not fully understand the associated risks.

Moreover, decentralization can foster an environment where investors, exposed to community information or popular trends, make impulsive decisions based on others' influence rather than rational analysis. The phenomenon of "herd mentality" is especially prevalent in these environments, where participants are drawn to others' decisions without adequately considering the fundamentals of the asset they are investing in. This can be exacerbated by the lack of regulation, which limits traditional tools for investor oversight and protection. Consequently, behavioral decisions in decentralized environments are influenced not only by individual psychological factors but also by group dynamics, potentially leading to speculative bubbles and increased market volatility.

PART IV: THE FUTURE OF BEHAVIORAL FINANCE

AI as an Architect of Financial Behavior

In the 21st century, artificial intelligence (AI) has disrupted finance, transforming how decisions are made and risks are managed. Beyond traditional quantitative analysis, AI now serves as a powerful tool for understanding and, in some cases, shaping financial behavior. With the ability to process vast amounts of data in real time, identify hidden patterns, and personalize strategies, AI is positioning itself as the architect of a new financial paradigm.

Emotional Algorithms

One of the most prominent advances of AI in finance is sentiment analysis, which uses advanced algorithms to interpret emotions, attitudes, and opinions expressed in text, such as news, social media posts, or conference transcripts. These tools provide investors with an edge by capturing early signals of market shifts that traditional analyses might overlook.

For instance, an algorithm can analyze thousands of Twitter posts about a specific company, detect a surge in negative comments, and predict a potential drop in its stock price before it happens. This approach enables fund managers to anticipate market movements, optimize portfolios, and mitigate risks.

Moreover, "emotional algorithms" go beyond passive sentiment analysis. These systems are designed to incorporate human behavioral models, such as risk aversion or overconfidence, into simulations and strategies. For example, an algorithm could automatically adjust a portfolio to reduce exposure to volatile assets during periods of high uncertainty, accounting for investors' heightened sensitivity to losses during such times.

However, this ability to model emotions also raises ethical concerns. To what extent is it appropriate to design strategies that exploit investors' behavioral biases? This dilemma highlights the need for proper regulation to balance innovation with user protection.

New Applications of Emotional Algorithms

Emotional algorithms are finding new applications beyond traditional sentiment analysis. One notable use is predicting financial crises by detecting large-scale emotional patterns. For example, a massive analysis of financial panic reflected in social media posts or news headlines can provide early warnings of drastic market movements. These tools not only anticipate changes but also allow fund managers to prepare for adverse scenarios before their effects materialize.

Additionally, their real-time capabilities optimize decision-making under high volatility conditions. By integrating emotional data from multiple sources within milliseconds, these systems can automatically adjust portfolios or strategies. For instance, if the analysis detects a sudden shift in global risk perception, it could reallocate assets to protect the investor, combining emotional intelligence with operational speed.

Beyond crisis prediction, these algorithms are starting to play a crucial role in identifying emerging opportunities in non-traditional markets. In developing economies, sentiment analysis can identify growing confidence in specific sectors or geographic regions, enabling early and strategic investments. This is transforming how risks and opportunities are assessed, providing competitive advantages to those who adopt this technology at early stages.

Multimodal Integration

One of the most significant advancements in emotional algorithms is their ability to integrate data from diverse modalities. They analyze not only text but also images and videos to gain a more comprehensive understanding of the emotions influencing the market. For example, an algorithm could analyze executives' speeches to detect signals of confidence or insecurity in their body language and tone of voice. By combining these cues with text analysis, the systems achieve far more accurate and contextual predictions.

This multimodal integration also enables broader coverage of events impacting the market. AI can process streams of data from social media, live news, and conference videos simultaneously, offering a holistic real-time view. This not only enriches investment strategies but also minimizes the risk of relying solely on one type of emotional data.

Another key advantage of multimodal integration is its ability to reduce biases in analyses. By combining multiple data sources, such as text, images, and audio, algorithms minimize the risks associated with one-dimensional interpretations. For example, a news article written in a neutral tone but accompanied by a video showing the speaker's alarmed expressions could trigger risk alerts that might otherwise go unnoticed. This holistic approach is particularly valuable in markets characterized by volatility and uncertainty.

Technical Advances

The development of emotional algorithms has been driven by advances in technologies like deep learning and natural language processing (NLP). These techniques enable the interpretation of complex emotions and linguistic nuances that were previously inaccessible to traditional systems. For instance, models like transformers, which are included in advanced AI tools, have revolutionized the ability to analyze sarcasm, irony, or emotional ambivalence in financial texts.

Generative models are also starting to play a crucial role in emotional algorithms. These systems not only predict emotions but also generate hypothetical scenarios simulating how markets might react to different events. For example, they could model the impact of an unexpected economic policy or a geopolitical crisis, providing investors with a framework to assess risks and opportunities.

These technical advances benefit not only large investors but also democratize access to sophisticated financial tools. Investment platforms are incorporating these models into applications targeting small and medium-sized investors, enabling them to make more informed and competitive decisions. This marks a shift toward a more inclusive financial ecosystem, where emotional analysis is no longer an exclusive privilege of large institutions.

Impact on Investor Psychology

The use of emotional algorithms is directly impacting investor psychology, altering how they perceive and react to the market. On the one hand, these systems help investors make more informed decisions by filtering emotional noise and providing objective analyses. On the other hand, their ability to influence market perception can create feedback loops, where emotion-based predictions reinforce collective behaviors like panic or euphoria.

This phenomenon raises questions about the sustainability of these tools in the long run. While they optimize portfolio management and mitigate risks, they could also foster greater dependency on algorithms, reducing investors' ability to make independent decisions. Thus, it is essential to balance their use with a critical approach that considers both their benefits and potential psychological consequences.

An interesting aspect of the psychological impact is how these algorithms can help investors overcome their own behavioral biases. By identifying repetitive emotional patterns in decision-making, these tools can offer personalized recommendations to improve investment strategies. This not only optimizes financial performance but also fosters greater self-awareness and emotional control among market participants.

Evolution Toward Personalization

One of the most promising trends in emotional algorithms is their evolution toward personalization. Instead of applying generic strategies, these systems are beginning to adapt to each investor's emotional profile and historical behavior. For example, an algorithm could identify that an investor is prone to overconfidence during boom periods and adjust strategies to counteract this bias, protecting their profitability.

Personalization also opens new opportunities in the WealthTech industry, enabling financial platforms to offer recommendations based on each user's specific emotions and goals. However, this level of adaptation raises ethical challenges, especially if personalized strategies end up exploiting investors' behavioral biases for the benefit of financial intermediaries.

Personalization is also paving the way for new horizons in risk management. By understanding investors' emotions and preferences, algorithms can design strategies aligned not only with financial objectives but also with their stress tolerance and reactions to losses. This approach not only improves financial outcomes but also strengthens the relationship between users and investment platforms, fostering greater trust and loyalty.

Successes and Failures

The success of emotional algorithms in the market already includes notable examples. In some cases, these tools have anticipated significant asset price changes by identifying early emotional trends in social media or news. For instance, analyzing negative sentiment toward a company on Twitter can alert investors to a drop in its stock price before traditional indicators react.

However, not all cases have been successful. Emotional algorithms can fail when interpreting ambiguous data or relying too heavily on a single information source. For example, these systems might overestimate the importance of a media event, generating false alarms that lead to inefficient investment decisions. This balance between success and failure underscores the need for a critical approach and the integration of multiple analytical methods.

Analyzing successes and failures also highlights the importance of data quality and diversity. Systems fed with biased or limited sources face a higher risk of producing erroneous results, underscoring the need for robust data collection and validation approaches. This reinforces the idea that the success of emotional algorithms depends not only on their design but also on the data infrastructure supporting them.

Broader Ethical Debate

The use of emotional algorithms raises significant ethical dilemmas. A central concern is their potential to manipulate markets through emotion analysis. For instance, organized campaigns flooding social media with fake news could exploit these systems to create artificial movements in asset prices.

Moreover, there is the risk that these algorithms disproportionately benefit large investors or financial institutions, exacerbating inequalities in access to advanced tools. This underscores the need for regulation to ensure the ethical and transparent use of these systems, protecting both individual investors and market integrity.

Ethical concerns also arise regarding how these systems may affect user privacy. Collecting emotional data, especially on public platforms like social media, raises questions about consent and the appropriate use of information. Balancing technological innovation with the protection of individual rights is essential, particularly in contexts where algorithms influence critical financial decisions.

The Future of Emotional Algorithms

The future of emotional algorithms promises revolutionary advancements, especially with the rise of technologies like quantum computing. These tools could model long-term emotional patterns in specific markets, enabling more precise anticipation and robust strategies. For example, a quantum system could analyze complex interactions among thousands of emotional factors to predict market reactions in high-uncertainty scenarios.

However, such progress also brings significant challenges. As emotional algorithms grow more sophisticated, implementing regulations to prevent misuse and ensure ethical operation will be crucial. This will not only protect investors but also ensure that financial markets remain fair and sustainable environments.

An intriguing future development is the potential collaboration of these algorithms with general artificial intelligence (AGI) systems, combining emotional analysis with broader predictive capabilities. This could revolutionize not only finance but also related fields such as behavioral economics and public policy management. However, the success of these integrations will depend on the design of interfaces between technologies and the regulations ensuring their responsible use.

Conclusion

Emotional algorithms represent a paradigm shift in modern finance, integrating sentiment analysis, human behavior models, and technical advancements to redefine decision-making in volatile and interconnected markets. Their ability to interpret emotions at scale, predict crises, and personalize strategies offers immense potential for investors and asset managers. However, these advancements come with ethical and technical challenges that require proper regulation and conscientious use.

The future of emotional algorithms is poised to be even more transformative, with applications that could extend beyond finance to fields such as psychology, economics, and politics. Along this journey, balancing innovation and ethics will be critical to ensuring that these tools not only benefit their users but also contribute to the sustainability and fairness of global markets. Emotional algorithms are not just tools; they are a bridge to a new era in the relationship between technology and human behavior.

Personalizing Financial Strategies with AI

Personalization is another area where AI is transforming finance. AI-based systems can analyze individual data such as financial goals, risk tolerance, investment history, and online behavior to design highly tailored strategies.

For instance, an AI-powered digital financial advisor could recommend a specific asset mix for a young investor prioritizing long-term growth, while suggesting a more conservative strategy for a retiree seeking to preserve capital. This personalization even extends to communication: some algorithms adjust the tone and frequency of client interactions based on their preferences and level of expertise.

Additionally, these tools are integrating gamification mechanisms to encourage positive financial behaviors. For example, an app might use personalized reminders and symbolic rewards to motivate users to save more or invest consistently, addressing issues like financial procrastination.

However, AI-driven personalization also faces challenges. One major concern is the risk of creating "decision bubbles," where users are exposed only to options aligned with their previous preferences, limiting their exposure to new perspectives and opportunities. This phenomenon, akin to confirmation bias on social media, could lead to suboptimal decisions or reinforce poor financial habits.

AI is not only shaping individual behavior but also influencing collective market behavior. With the proliferation of algorithms responding to real-time data, financial markets have become more reactive and, in some cases, more volatile. A clear example is the phenomenon of flash crashes, where high-frequency trading algorithms amplify rapid price drops.

However, the same AI contributing to these disruptions can also offer solutions. Regulators are beginning to use AI to monitor and mitigate systemic risks, analyzing vast volumes of market data for signs of manipulation or instability.

Evolution Toward Hyper-Personalization

Hyper-personalization represents the next level of AI-driven financial transformation. Instead of offering general recommendations based on static profiles, algorithms now incorporate dynamic, real-time analyses, including macroeconomic data, market indicators, and relevant news events. For example, a system can automatically adjust equity exposure upon detecting increased market volatility, combining this information with the user's risk tolerance.

Moreover, this technology enables a proactive approach. Rather than reacting to past events, AI can anticipate trends by analyzing historical patterns and data correlations. This not only enhances the accuracy of financial strategies but also helps users quickly adapt to changing environments, maximizing returns and minimizing risks.

Nonetheless, hyper-personalization raises concerns regarding privacy and data management. As algorithms access an increasing amount of personal and contextual information, robust security measures must be implemented, and users must understand how their data is being used. Trust in these platforms will be essential for widespread adoption.

Collaborative Personalization

Collaborative personalization combines the strengths of AI's advanced data analysis with human empathy. Financial advisors can now use AI tools to gain quick and accurate insights, such as identifying emerging trends or assessing complex risks, while maintaining their ability to emotionally connect with clients. This is particularly important when users require emotional guidance in addition to data-driven insights.

For example, during periods of high economic uncertainty, such as recessions or financial crises, an advisor could use AI to project alternative scenarios and illustrate potential portfolio impacts. They can then complement these analyses with clear explanations and personalized advice, helping clients make informed decisions without feeling overwhelmed.

This collaboration also enhances the accessibility of financial services. AI systems can handle routine tasks, freeing up time for human advisors to focus on more meaningful interactions. This ensures that even users with smaller portfolios can access advanced advisory levels, promoting broader financial inclusion.

Impact on Financial Education

AI-powered personalization is revolutionizing how people learn about finance. Algorithms can identify gaps in users' financial knowledge and provide educational content tailored to their needs. For instance, a user frequently making impulsive investment decisions might receive tutorials on diversification and risk management, based on their history and preferences.

Furthermore, platforms are leveraging practical simulations as learning tools. These allow users to experiment with investment strategies in virtual environments before applying them in real life. By offering an interactive and personalized experience, these tools improve users' technical knowledge and confidence in making informed decisions.

This educational approach has long-term positive effects on financial behavior. By equipping users with practical skills and specific knowledge, platforms encourage more responsible and less impulsive decision-making. This not only benefits individuals but also contributes to overall market stability by reducing extreme and irrational behaviors.

New Opportunities for Financial Inclusion

AI-driven personalization is playing a crucial role in financial inclusion, enabling more people to access services previously reserved for large investors. Micro-investment tools and robo-advisors use algorithms to design accessible strategies tailored to the needs and capabilities of small savers. This democratizes access to financial markets, encouraging greater participation.

For instance, a person with limited resources can use an app that recommends fractional investments in stocks or ETFs based on their monthly savings capacity. These apps simplify the experience, removing traditional barriers like complex financial jargon or high entry costs, fostering long-term saving and investment habits.

Financial inclusion extends beyond individual users. Many platforms are designing specific solutions for small and medium-sized enterprises, helping them access financing and manage resources more efficiently. AI personalizes these services by assessing each business's financial situation and offering tailored solutions, from credit lines to cash flow optimization strategies.

Regulation and Ethics in Personalization

The growing personalization also brings ethical and regulatory challenges that cannot be overlooked. AI platforms must ensure their recommendations are unbiased and prioritize users' interests over commercial incentives. For example, a digital advisor should not favor products with higher commissions if they are not the most suitable for the client.

Transparency is also critical. Users need to understand how and why recommendations are generated. This includes explaining the data models used and the assumptions behind suggested strategies. Greater clarity in this regard not only strengthens user trust but also helps mitigate risks associated with poorly informed decisions.

Regulation plays a vital role in ensuring these platforms operate fairly and responsibly. Policymakers must collaborate with AI and financial experts to develop frameworks that balance technological innovation with consumer protection, fostering a more ethical and sustainable financial ecosystem.

Closing Thoughts

Artificial intelligence is redefining the rules of finance, providing tools to understand and optimize financial behavior at both individual and collective levels. From emotional algorithms capturing market sentiment nuances to personalized strategies adapting solutions to investors' unique needs, AI is laying the foundation for a smarter, more accessible financial future.

However, this technological revolution is not without challenges. Ethical concerns, volatility risks, and potential inequalities in access to these technologies must be addressed to ensure AI becomes a force for good in global finance. As an architect of financial behavior, AI has the potential to build a more efficient and equitable system, provided it is used responsibly and with a long-term vision.

Towards a New Paradigm: Cognitive Finance

The evolution of behavioral finance is reaching a new threshold, where the integration of artificial intelligence (AI) with neuroeconomics is shaping what some experts call cognitive finance. This emerging approach combines advanced technological tools with a deeper understanding of the human brain and decision-making processes, promising to revolutionize financial markets and individual behaviors.

AI and Neuroeconomics

Neuroeconomics, which studies how brain structures and processes influence economic decisions, has been a field of interest since the pioneering work of Kahneman and Tversky. Now, integration with AI amplifies this field by enabling more detailed and dynamic analyses of human behavior.

For instance, devices that measure brain activity, such as electroencephalograms (EEG) and functional magnetic resonance imaging (fMRI), generate vast amounts of data that AI algorithms can process. These models identify patterns in individuals' emotional and cognitive responses to economic stimuli, such as financial risks or savings incentives.

A practical example is the development of investment strategies based on investors' neural activity. By analyzing how the brain responds to fear or euphoria during market fluctuations, AI-based tools can anticipate impulsive decisions and suggest interventions to mitigate biases, such as panic selling or overinvesting in trendy assets.

Moreover, AI-assisted neuroeconomics contributes to the more effective design of financial nudges. By identifying which stimuli are most effective at activating brain areas associated with self-control or reward, algorithms enable the creation of strategies that promote more rational and sustainable behaviors.

Predictive Models Based on Brain Activity

The integration of AI with neural data has led to predictive models capable of anticipating how people will react to various economic stimuli. These models process data from tools like EEG and fMRI to identify correlations between brain activity patterns and economic behaviors, such as risk aversion, impulsivity, or saving tendencies. This allows researchers to better understand how emotional and cognitive factors shape financial decisions.

One practical example is using these models to predict market behavior during periods of high uncertainty, such as economic crises. Algorithms can identify neural signals associated with fear or confidence, providing risk managers and analysts valuable insights to anticipate market movements. This approach not only enhances the accuracy of economic forecasts but also enables the design of more effective risk mitigation strategies.

At the individual level, these models can personalize financial recommendations. For example, if an algorithm detects that a person tends to make impulsive decisions under stress, it might suggest tools that encourage a more reflective approach, such as waiting periods before confirming investments. This could transform how consumers interact with their finances, promoting more deliberate decisions aligned with long-term goals.

Personalizing Economic Experiences

The combination of neuroeconomics and AI is redefining how people experience and manage their interaction with financial services. By analyzing neural data in real time, platforms can adapt their design and content to the cognitive and emotional needs of each user. For instance, a digital banking application might automatically adjust the amount of information presented if it detects signs of stress or mental overload, facilitating a smoother and more efficient experience.

In the realm of financial education, these technologies allow for personalized teaching methods. A system could monitor users' attention and comprehension levels, providing more detailed explanations or practical examples when difficulties are detected. This approach not only enhances knowledge retention but also motivates users by tailoring learning to their pace and style.

On a broader scale, these capabilities can be applied to design more inclusive marketing campaigns and financial products. For example, insurers could develop personalized plans based on each client's risk tolerance, while credit institutions might offer rates adapted to psychological profiles, reducing default risks. This fosters a more balanced and trustworthy relationship between consumers and financial institutions.

Ethics and Privacy in Neuroeconomics and AI

The use of neural data combined with AI raises significant ethical dilemmas, particularly regarding consent and privacy. Unlike other types of data, brain patterns are extremely sensitive as they reflect emotional states and internal thoughts. Without adequate regulatory frameworks, there is a risk that this information could be used to manipulate economic decisions or create psychological profiles without users' knowledge or consent.

Additionally, the ability to influence financial decisions through personalized stimuli also raises concerns. While these tools can promote positive behaviors, such as saving or planning, they could also be used to maximize corporate profits at the expense of consumers by exploiting biases like overconfidence or fear of missing out. Such practices could exacerbate economic inequalities and erode trust in institutions.

To address these challenges, it is crucial to establish regulations that ensure transparency and accountability in the use of neural data. Companies and organizations must implement clear mechanisms for informed consent and limit access to this information. Furthermore, educating the public about the benefits and risks associated with these technologies will be essential to promoting an ethical and equitable use of AI-assisted neuroeconomics.

In Summary

The convergence of artificial intelligence and neuroeconomics is redefining our understanding of human behavior and its impact on economic decisions. From predictive models based on neural data to deeply personalized financial experiences, these technologies offer unprecedented transformative potential. However, this advancement also raises ethical questions and challenges related to privacy, consent, and the fair use of sensitive information.

To responsibly harness these opportunities, it will be essential to combine technological innovation with robust regulations that protect users and promote transparency. Additionally, educating the public and key players in the financial sector about the benefits and risks of these tools will help build trust and encourage their ethical adoption. Ultimately, the integration of AI and neuroeconomics has the potential not only to optimize financial strategies but also to empower individuals in their relationship with the economy, provided that a balance between innovation and responsibility is maintained.

AI-driven automation is redefining how individuals interact with the financial world. Robo-advisors, for instance, have streamlined investment management by automating complex tasks such as portfolio diversification and asset rebalancing. However, these tools impact not only technical decisions but also how users perceive risk, trust, and their own control over their finances.

Delegation and Emotional Connection

One key aspect is how automation influences the perception of responsibility. Recent studies suggest that people tend to delegate more decisions to machines in high-uncertainty contexts, reducing stress associated with complex decision-making. Yet, this delegation can also lead to emotional detachment, making users less likely to learn from their mistakes or grasp the long-term consequences of their choices.

Amplifying and Mitigating Biases

Automated decisions can magnify pre-existing biases. For example, if an algorithm prioritizes assets with high historical performance, it could reinforce the availability bias, leading investors to overvalue popular options while underestimating less visible but equally viable alternatives. This raises questions about designing systems that are not only technically accurate but also behaviorally ethical.

On the other hand, AI advancements offer opportunities to counteract biases proactively. Personalized financial platforms can identify behavioral patterns and provide recommendations that help users overcome counterproductive tendencies, such as saving more consistently or avoiding impulsive decisions during market downturns.

Toward Balanced Human-Machine Interaction

The fusion of cognitive finance and AI opens the door to a collaborative model between humans and machines. Rather than replacing human intuition, these technologies aim to complement it, enabling more informed and strategic decision-making. This approach requires renewed financial education, teaching users not only to utilize advanced tools but also to understand their limitations and associated risks.

The Role of Trust and Transparency

Trust is essential for users to adopt and rely on automated financial decisions. If algorithms are not transparent about their decision-making processes, users may feel insecure and hesitant to entrust their finances. Transparency in how automated systems select investments, assess risks, or make adjustments is crucial to ensuring users understand the rationale behind decisions. Without clear explanations, trust can erode, hindering widespread acceptance of these tools.

Beyond explaining algorithms, transparency also involves ethical and secure handling of personal and financial data. Platforms must provide clear, comprehensible explanations of their recommendations and decisions, fostering an environment of trust where users feel informed and confident.

Personalization and Dynamic Adjustment

Personalization is a groundbreaking aspect of automated decisions, enabling financial strategies tailored to each user's needs and behaviors. However, the real advantage of automation lies in its ability to dynamically adjust to market changes and users' personal circumstances. AI algorithms can analyze vast amounts of data, including past behaviors, preferences, emotional reactions, and long-term goals, to make automatic adjustments to investment portfolios.

Dynamic adjustment is particularly relevant during significant economic events, such as market downturns or sudden interest rate changes. For instance, during a financial crisis, algorithms could automatically mitigate risk based on users' previous behavior patterns, such as risk aversion to volatility. This capability helps users maintain a balanced, rational approach over time, fostering more stable financial management.

Closing Thoughts

The convergence of neuroeconomics and artificial intelligence is transforming finance by combining deep insights into human behavior with the analytical power of technology. This paradigm shift not only promises greater efficiency and precision in markets but also addresses behavioral challenges that have long puzzled investors.

However, the journey toward cognitive finance also entails ethical, technical, and social challenges. Unlocking its full potential will require balancing innovation with a strong commitment to responsibility, ensuring that this transformation serves not only markets but also the broader well-being of individuals and communities.

The Impact of Automated Decisions on Behavior

AI-driven automation is redefining how individuals interact with the financial world. Robo-advisors, for instance, have streamlined investment management by automating complex tasks such as portfolio diversification and asset rebalancing. However, these tools impact not only technical decisions but also how users perceive risk, trust, and their own control over their finances.

Delegation and Emotional Connection

One key aspect is how automation influences the perception of responsibility. Recent studies suggest that people tend to delegate more decisions to machines in high-uncertainty contexts, reducing stress associated with complex decision-making. Yet, this delegation can also lead to emotional detachment, making users less likely to learn from their mistakes or grasp the long-term consequences of their choices.

Amplifying and Mitigating Biases

Automated decisions can magnify pre-existing biases. For example, if an algorithm prioritizes assets with high historical performance, it could reinforce the availability bias, leading investors to overvalue popular options while underestimating less visible but equally viable alternatives. This raises questions about designing systems that are not only technically accurate but also behaviorally ethical.

On the other hand, AI advancements offer opportunities to counteract biases proactively. Personalized financial platforms can identify behavioral patterns and provide recommendations that help users overcome counterproductive tendencies, such as saving more consistently or avoiding impulsive decisions during market downturns.

Toward Balanced Human-Machine Interaction

The fusion of cognitive finance and AI opens the door to a collaborative model between humans and machines. Rather than replacing human intuition, these technologies aim to complement it, enabling more informed and strategic decision-making. This approach requires renewed financial education, teaching users not only to utilize advanced tools but also to understand their limitations and associated risks.

The Role of Trust and Transparency

Trust is essential for users to adopt and rely on automated financial decisions. If algorithms are not transparent about their decision-making processes, users may feel insecure and hesitant to entrust their finances. Transparency in how automated systems select investments, assess risks, or make adjustments is crucial to ensuring users understand the rationale behind decisions. Without clear explanations, trust can erode, hindering widespread acceptance of these tools.

Beyond explaining algorithms, transparency also involves ethical and secure handling of personal and financial data. Platforms must provide clear, comprehensible explanations of their recommendations and decisions, fostering an environment of trust where users feel informed and confident.

Personalization and Dynamic Adjustment

Personalization is a groundbreaking aspect of automated decisions, enabling financial strategies tailored to each user's needs and behaviors. However, the real advantage of automation lies in its ability to dynamically adjust to market changes and users' personal circumstances. AI algorithms can analyze vast amounts of data, including past behaviors, preferences, emotional reactions, and long-term goals, to make automatic adjustments to investment portfolios.

Dynamic adjustment is particularly relevant during significant economic events, such as market downturns or sudden interest rate changes. For instance, during a financial crisis, algorithms could automatically mitigate risk based on users' previous behavior patterns, such as risk aversion to volatility. This capability helps users maintain a balanced, rational approach over time, fostering more stable financial management.

Conclusion

The convergence of neuroeconomics and artificial intelligence is transforming finance by combining deep insights into human behavior with the analytical power of technology. This paradigm shift not only promises greater efficiency and precision in markets but also addresses behavioral challenges that have long puzzled investors.

However, the journey toward cognitive finance also entails ethical, technical, and social challenges. Unlocking its full potential will require balancing innovation with a strong commitment to responsibility, ensuring that this transformation serves not only markets but also the broader well-being of individuals and communities.

Ethics and Regulation in an Automated Financial World

As finance evolves toward an automated model driven by artificial intelligence (AI) and behavioral analysis, ethical and regulatory issues are taking center stage. These technologies are not only transforming the dynamics of markets but also how individuals make financial decisions. While these innovations promise efficiency and personalization, they also pose significant risks related to manipulation, inequality, and lack of transparency.

Risks of Behavior Manipulation

One of the main ethical challenges of financial automation is the potential to manipulate users' behavior. AI-powered platforms, by analyzing massive datasets, can identify specific behavioral vulnerabilities and design strategies to exploit them. For example:

- **Inducing Debt**: Credit platforms can use AI to identify users prone to impulsive decisions, offering them seemingly attractive terms that end up trapping them in unsustainable debt cycles.

- **Overconfidence in Algorithms**: Users may delegate critical decisions to systems that prioritize the provider's commercial benefit over the customer's well-being. This occurs when an algorithm suggests high-risk investments disguised as optimal solutions.

- **Induced Consumption**: On platforms combining financial services with e-commerce, like certain digital wallets, digital nudges may encourage users to spend more rather than save, appealing to their emotional biases.

These cases reveal an ethical dilemma: while designers of automated financial systems have the power to positively influence financial behaviors, they can also abuse this influence to maximize short-term profits, sacrificing users' financial sustainability.

The risk of manipulation is also related to the lack of transparency in how algorithms make decisions. Users may be led to make financial choices they don't fully understand, increasing the likelihood of mistakes or suboptimal decisions. Personalization offered through AI, while beneficial in terms of adaptability, can be used to exploit users' cognitive weaknesses. By hiding or disguising key information behind recommendations, platforms could be violating fundamental principles of financial ethics, such as honesty and clarity. This could lead to a power imbalance, where users, unable to understand the underlying algorithms, are forced to blindly trust automated decisions.

Moreover, behavioral manipulation not only affects individuals but can have systemic consequences. If platforms begin using aggressive persuasion tactics to maximize commercial profit, they could contribute to the creation of financial bubbles or amplify risky behaviors in markets. This is particularly dangerous in emerging or highly volatile markets, where less informed investors are more vulnerable. In these contexts, AI could encourage reckless speculation, affecting not only individuals but also the stability of the financial system in general. Therefore, the regulation and ethical oversight of automated technologies are crucial to ensure that AI is used for the common good and not to maximize profit at the expense of users' financial well-being.

Regulatory Challenges at the Convergence of AI and Finance

The convergence of advanced technologies and financial markets presents complex regulatory challenges, where traditional oversight approaches are insufficient to address emerging issues. Some of the main challenges include:

1. **Algorithm Transparency**: Automated financial decisions are often based on AI models that function as "black boxes." This means that even their developers may not always be able to explain how an algorithm arrived at a specific decision. This level of opacity makes accountability difficult and generates distrust among users. Regulations should require greater clarity in the design and functioning of algorithms.

2. **Data Protection**: The massive collection of personal data to feed AI models raises privacy concerns. It is essential to establish limits on what data can be collected, how it is stored, and who has access to it, especially in a financial context where sensitive information may be exploited for manipulation.

3. **Algorithmic Discrimination**: Biases in training data can lead to financial decisions that perpetuate or even exacerbate inequality. For example, credit-determining algorithms may discriminate against certain demographic groups based on historical exclusion patterns. Regulations must ensure that AI systems are audited to prevent such injustices.

4. **Accountability for Systemic Failures**: As more critical decisions are delegated to AI, the question arises: who is responsible when a system fails? Regulations must clearly define the responsibilities of developers, users, and financial entities to avoid legal gaps in crisis situations.

Towards a Balanced Ethical and Regulatory Framework

Designing an ethical and regulatory framework that encompasses financial automation requires close collaboration between regulators, technologists, and market players. Some key principles include:

- **Promoting Financial and Digital Literacy**: Users should understand how automated platforms work, their benefits, and their risks. Financial and digital literacy is essential to empower individuals in the face of these new challenges.

- **Promoting Ethics by Design**: Financial systems should be designed from the outset with clear ethical principles, prioritizing sustainability and user well-being over short-term commercial benefits.

- **Adopting Dynamic Regulations**: Regulations must evolve alongside technologies, avoiding gaps that could be exploited by unscrupulous actors. This includes creating specialized agencies for overseeing emerging technologies in finance.

Moreover, the rapid pace at which AI is evolving presents a unique challenge for regulation. Traditional regulatory frameworks are not designed to adapt to the speed of technological innovation. While AI can learn and adapt quickly, laws and regulations tend to be more rigid and slow to implement. This creates a regulatory gap that can be exploited by those seeking to circumvent oversight. Therefore, regulatory authorities must be more agile and proactive, working in collaboration with tech companies to anticipate risks before they materialize, rather than reacting only when problems have already occurred.

The financial sector is especially sensitive to automation, as erroneous or manipulative decisions can have wider repercussions, affecting the stability of the global market. Therefore, regulatory policies must not only focus on data security and privacy but also on the social and economic impact of automated decisions. Regulation should ensure that AI in the financial sector is not only transparent and fair but also promotes greater financial inclusion. In this regard, policies must focus on reducing technological and educational barriers that could leave certain groups behind, ensuring that the benefits of AI are accessible to all, not just a privileged few.

Chapter Conclusion

The rise of automated, AI-driven finance presents unprecedented opportunities but also demands a solid ethical and regulatory approach to prevent abuses and inequalities. Ultimately, the success of this transformation will depend on our ability to balance innovation with responsibility, building systems that not only optimize financial performance but also reflect broader social values such as equity, transparency, and respect for individual rights.

The path toward an automated financial future must be guided by a vision that prioritizes collective well-being, where new technologies benefit not only those who have access to them but also close inequality gaps and provide opportunities to all sectors of society. While advancements in AI have the potential to make financial systems more efficient and accessible, the vulnerability of users to algorithmic biases and behavioral manipulation remains a central concern. The key will be ensuring that regulations evolve alongside technology, creating a robust oversight framework that maintains a balance between innovation and social justice.

Additionally, financial and digital literacy will be crucial to empower individuals in this new context. For users to make informed decisions, they must understand not only the benefits of automated tools but also the inherent risks of using them. Only through an ethical, inclusive, and educational approach can we ensure that AI-driven automated finance contributes to a more just and sustainable economic system for all, where technology serves as a means to improve quality of life rather than deepening pre-existing inequalities.

PART V: FROM THEORY TO PRACTICE: REAL-WORLD APPLICATIONS

Investor Behavior in Real Scenarios

In a world where financial decisions are increasingly influenced by emotions, cognitive biases, and emerging technologies, the challenge for academics and professionals is not only to understand the principles of behavioral finance but also to apply them effectively. This part of the book seeks to bridge the gap between theory and practice, providing tools and approaches that enable the application of behavioral finance concepts in the classroom, businesses, and markets.

Teaching behavioral finance requires a dynamic approach that combines real-world cases, simulations, and critical analysis of the biases that shape human decisions. On the other hand, financial companies face the challenge of integrating these ideas into their daily operations, whether to design more effective strategies or to promote an ethical and transparent environment in their interactions with clients.

Throughout this section, we will explore how financial executives, educators, and practitioners in general can employ behavioral principles to transform the way finance is applied. From pedagogical methodologies to innovative business strategies, this part offers a practical framework for turning knowledge into real impact.

1. **How to Interpret Market Sentiment Indices**

    A market sentiment index reflects the dominant emotions among participants (optimism, fear, euphoria, etc.) and can be derived from surveys, social media analysis, trading volume, or even news headlines.

    Practical Use:

- Identify moments of euphoria (bubble peaks) or panic (buying opportunities).
- Complement technical and fundamental analysis to refine entry and exit decisions.
- Common tools: the Fear and Greed Index (CNN), volatility indices (VIX), and Big Data-based measurements.

Practical Example: During the cryptocurrency boom, sentiment analysis showed optimism spikes just before major crashes, as seen in 2017 and 2021.

Integrating sentiment indices into financial decision-making can provide a crucial strategic advantage, especially in complex markets. By combining these indicators with technical and fundamental approaches, investors can build a more complete view, reduce unnecessary risks, and seize opportunities that might otherwise go unnoticed.

2. **Behavioral Decisions in Emerging Markets**

Emerging markets represent a complex and challenging environment for investors. With characteristics such as high volatility, sensitivity to external factors, and a profile of local investors influenced by specific behavioral biases, these economies present both significant challenges and unique opportunities. In this context, understanding human behavior and cultural particularities becomes essential for navigating inherent risks and capitalizing on strategic entry points.

Through adapted strategies, it is possible not only to mitigate the adverse effects of uncertainty but also to identify innovative solutions that capitalize on the dynamics of these economies.

Unique Characteristics:
- ✓ Higher volatility due to economic and political instability.

- ✓ Greater sensitivity to external events (interest rates in the U.S., commodity prices).
- ✓ Local investors tend to show biases such as home bias or extreme risk aversion.

Key Strategies:
- ✓ Incorporate crisis scenarios into financial planning.
- ✓ Design financial products tailored to risk aversion (e.g., currency hedge funds).
- ✓ Analyze cultural narratives influencing decisions.

In emerging markets, recognizing the particularities of investor behavior is essential for designing effective strategies. By adapting financial tools to local sensitivities and the political-economic context, risks can be mitigated and unique opportunities can be seized that, although challenging, can be highly profitable for well-prepared actors.

3. **The Role of "Narrative Analysis" in Investing**

In the financial world, the stories told about markets, industries, or assets have a remarkable power to influence investment decisions. These narratives, built around ideas such as the rise of disruptive technologies, the recovery of specific sectors, or the imminent collapse of certain assets, can be as influential as the numbers in financial reports.

Narrative analysis emerges as a key tool for understanding and predicting market movements. Beyond identifying which stories dominate at any given time, this approach allows for evaluating their potential impact and discerning between grounded and speculative narratives. This section discusses how to leverage this tool to make more informed and strategic investment decisions.

What is it?

Investment is not only guided by numbers but by the stories the markets create: "The rise of AI," "The fall of the dollar," etc. These narratives shape expectations and decisions.

How to Leverage It:

- ✓ Evaluate dominant narratives in media and social networks to anticipate trends.
- ✓ Differentiate between grounded narratives (AI sector growth) and speculative ones (promises of unrealistic returns).
- ✓ **Example**: The narrative of "untouchable tech companies" was key in the dot-com bubble, while solid fundamentals supported stories like Amazon's.

Understanding and using narrative analysis as an investment tool allows market participants to separate fleeting trends from real opportunities. By identifying the most influential stories and evaluating their validity, investors can anticipate market movements more accurately and make more informed decisions in a financial environment where perceptions are as important as data.

Designing Behavioral Strategies for Investors and Companies

In the field of finance, personalized nudges have become a powerful tool to guide investors toward more rational decisions without restricting their freedom of choice. Inspired by principles of behavioral economics, these small "pushes" are designed to mitigate common biases and promote healthy financial habits. In this section, we will explore how automation, default diversification, and the analysis of historical behavior can be used to improve investment portfolio management.

What are nudges?

Small psychological pushes that guide investors toward more rational decisions without restricting their freedom.

Practical applications:

- Automated saving and investing: Offering default options like automatic dividend reinvestment plans.
- Simplified diversification: Designing balanced portfolios by default to avoid overconfidence bias or preference for local assets.
- Analyzing previous behavior: Using historical client data to provide recommendations tailored to their emotional profile.
- Practical example: Vanguard and other asset managers use digital tools that suggest options based on the client's risk tolerance.

Personalized nudges represent a bridge between behavioral theory and financial practice, allowing portfolio managers to design strategies that align financial goals with the actual behaviors of investors. This symbiosis between technology, psychology, and finance not only enhances rational decision-making but also democratizes access to sophisticated financial solutions for a wider audience.

1. **Using AI Algorithms to Predict Behavior**

Advances in artificial intelligence have revolutionized the ability to analyze and predict behavior in the financial realm. By processing vast amounts of structured and unstructured data, machine learning algorithms identify behavioral patterns that allow for anticipating market reactions and optimizing investment decisions. This section examines the key applications of these algorithms, from predicting impulsive purchases to personalizing financial strategies.

How do they work?

Machine learning algorithms can analyze large volumes of data, from past transactions to social media activity, to identify behavioral patterns.

Key advantages:

- Forecasting peaks of impulsive buying or panic selling.
- Identifying undervalued assets through emotional analysis.
- Personalizing financial recommendations in real-time.
- Use case: A fintech company can analyze credit card data and consumer habits to suggest investments consistent with the customer's behavior.

Integrating AI algorithms into financial behavior analysis marks a paradigm shift in investment management. By combining emotional and behavioral data with quantitative predictions, institutions can offer more tailored and resilient solutions, contributing to an investment experience that blends cutting-edge technology with a deep understanding of human behavior.

2. Incorporating Emotional Analysis into Financial Plans

Emotion plays a central role in financial decisions, influencing everything from risk tolerance to responses to unexpected events. Incorporating emotional analysis into financial planning allows for anticipating irrational behaviors and building more robust and adaptable strategies. This section delves into the tools and methodologies that integrate emotions into financial planning, improving responsiveness in volatile contexts.

Emotion as a key variable

Financial decisions are deeply emotional. Incorporating emotional metrics helps anticipate irrational behaviors.

Practical tools:

- ✓ Surveys to measure risk tolerance in different scenarios (euphoria, panic).

- ✓ Tone analysis on social media and news related to specific assets.
- ✓ Measuring emotional volatility during periods of high uncertainty, such as elections or global crises.

Practical example: During the pandemic, many institutions adjusted their risk models to account for the emotional impact of collective fear on investment decisions.

Incorporating emotional analysis into financial plans goes beyond the traditional approach, allowing for a more holistic understanding of the investor. In a world where emotions can trigger significant market movements, this perspective becomes a key differentiator for creating more human and effective strategies.

Simulations and Learning Tools

In the financial field, simulations and learning tools have emerged as essential resources to understand the complex dynamics of markets and strengthen strategic decision-making. These methodologies allow students, academics, and professionals to experiment in controlled environments, replicating real-world scenarios without assuming significant risks. From the analysis of speculative bubbles to the implementation of hybrid models that combine traditional and behavioral finance, these tools offer a practical and enriching approach to developing analytical and strategic skills.

The use of interactive platforms, such as investment simulators and specialized software, fosters active learning focused on problem-solving. By combining theory with practice, these technologies not only prepare users to interpret market signals but also promote a deeper understanding of the emotional and rational factors that influence financial decisions.

As technology continues to transform the financial sector, simulations and learning tools have become a bridge between academic knowledge and the demands of the real world. This dynamic and versatile approach allows participants to acquire key competencies to face challenges in increasingly interconnected and volatile markets.

I. Interactive Case Studies to Understand Bubbles and Crashes

Historical events in financial markets offer a rich source of lessons on behavioral patterns that lead to speculative bubbles or sudden crashes. Through interactive case studies, participants can explore in detail how collective emotions, such as euphoria or panic, triggered these phenomena and how such dynamics can be recognized in real-time. These activities not only promote critical analysis but also prepare professionals to identify and respond to similar situations in the future.

- **Objective**: Analyze historical events in financial markets to identify behavioral patterns that lead to speculative bubbles or sudden crashes.

- **Available Tools**:
    - Platforms like TradingView or Bloomberg Terminal to recreate historical scenarios.
    - Academic simulators allowing exploration of decisions in real-time (e.g., Wharton Investment Simulator).

- **Practical Example**:
    - Review of the Dotcom Bubble (1999-2000): What behavioral signals, such as excessive optimism, predicted the crash?
    - Subprime Crisis (2008): Exploration of emotional contagion and mass sell-offs as triggers for the collapse.

Learning through interactive case studies provides invaluable experience for financial practitioners, combining theory and practice in a dynamic environment. This approach not only helps understand the past but also develops analytical skills to forecast and mitigate risks in complex scenarios, strengthening informed and resilient decision-making.

II. Hybrid Models: Combining Traditional and Behavioral Finance

The integration of traditional and behavioral finance represents a holistic approach to addressing the complexity of market behavior. While traditional finance focuses on quantitative metrics to assess risk and return, behavioral finance incorporates emotional and psychological factors that influence investor decisions. This hybrid model allows for the development of strategies that are not only technically sound but also adaptable to human nature.

- **Concept**: Traditional finance offers a logical framework for assessing risk and return, while behavioral finance helps interpret emotional deviations.

- **How to Integrate**:

Use traditional metrics like the CAPM to calculate expected return but adjust expectations considering biases like overconfidence or risk aversion.

Incorporate emotional volatility indices (such as the VIX) to refine portfolio management strategies.

- **Practical Example**:

A fund manager may adjust its allocation to volatile sectors (e.g., technology, cryptocurrencies) during periods of euphoria, using sentiment data to prevent excesses.

Adopting a hybrid approach to finance not only improves strategy accuracy but also fosters a more comprehensive understanding of markets. By balancing the logic of traditional models with the behavioral perspective, professionals can tackle investment challenges with greater agility and proactively respond to market fluctuations in an empathetic manner.

III. Recommended Software and Platforms for Professionals

In a world where technology and markets evolve rapidly, the use of specialized software has become indispensable for financial professionals. Tools like Sentifi, Koyfin, IBM Watson, and Refinitiv's Eikon combine technical and fundamental data analysis with emotional and sentiment perspectives, providing a strategic advantage to those seeking to navigate highly volatile environments successfully.

- **Featured Options**:

Sentifi: A sentiment analysis tool that combines social media, news, and financial data.

Koyfin: A platform for analyzing fundamental and technical data with a visual focus.

IBM Watson: AI integration for analyzing behavioral patterns in large databases.

Refinitiv Eikon: Tracks market trends and analyzes sentiment data in real-time.

- **Advantages of These Tools**:

Improve prediction capability. Help personalize strategies. Offer an integrated perspective by combining hard data with emotional analysis.

The incorporation of these technological platforms not only optimizes financial analysis but also raises the standard of strategic decision-making in the sector. By integrating quantitative and qualitative data, professionals can gain a more complete view of the market, personalize solutions, and stay ahead of emerging trends, strengthening their position in a competitive environment.

Real Case Studies and Practical Simulations

Real-world case studies and practical simulations have proven to be powerful tools for learning and applying financial concepts. Analyzing historical market events, such as speculative bubbles and economic crises, helps identify behavior patterns that led to key decisions, while simulations provide a safe space to experiment with strategies in real-time. This approach combines the rigor of theoretical analysis with practical experience, offering a comprehensive view of how rational and emotional factors shape markets.

1. Learning from Major Financial Bubbles

- **Purpose**: To use historical events to illustrate how cognitive and emotional biases contributed to market excesses and crises.

- **Notable examples**:

Tulip Mania (1637): One of the first documented bubbles, marked by irrational euphoria surrounding tulip bulbs.

1929 Stock Market Crash: Overconfidence and widespread use of leverage were key ingredients for the collapse.

Bitcoin in 2017: Overblown expectations about technological adoption fueled a cycle of euphoria and fear.

- **Lessons learned**:

Recognizing early signs of euphoria and excessive skepticism. Identifying how narratives drive investor behavior.

Analyzing major financial bubbles of the past not only provides valuable lessons but also helps develop a critical mindset for future market cycles. By understanding the mechanisms behind these crises, investors can adopt more informed strategies and avoid falling into repetitive behavioral patterns. Recognizing the impact of collective emotions and dominant narratives is key to preventing costly mistakes at both individual and institutional levels.

2. Designing Market Simulations for Behavioral Analysis

- **Practical tools**:

Creating simulated environments that allow participants to make financial decisions under uncertainty.

Incorporating variables such as price fluctuations, unexpected news, and regulatory changes.

- **Simulation example**:

Participants must manage a portfolio during a "bear market," facing dilemmas such as when to sell assets, diversify, or stay put.

Results highlight common biases like loss aversion and herd behavior.

Market simulations not only allow for evaluating decisions in a controlled environment but also foster awareness of the behavioral biases that affect decision-making. This practical approach helps participants develop more resilient and adaptive strategies in the face of uncertainty. Incorporating these lessons into professional training ensures better preparation to face the challenges of complex and ever-evolving markets.

3. Investors and Companies Facing Global Crises

- **Notable cases**:

COVID-19 Pandemic: How collective fear and uncertainty affected decision-making, from increased demand for safe-haven assets (gold, bonds) to the surge in tech stocks.

1973 Oil Crisis: Initial panic led to hasty investment decisions, while companies adapted long-term strategies.

Ukraine Invasion (2022): Unexpected changes in supply chains and volatility in energy markets tested resilience.

- **Key lessons**:

The importance of contingency plans and diversification.

Using sentiment analysis tools to anticipate changes in market behavior.

Global crises reveal the importance of preparedness, adaptability, and deep market behavior analysis. Both investors and companies must learn to integrate behavioral tools into their strategies to respond more effectively to volatility and uncertainty. Incorporating these lessons into financial planning not only helps mitigate risks but also identify opportunities amid adversity.

Ethics and Responsibility in Designing Behavioral Strategies

The design of behavioral strategies in the financial and business realms not only involves the use of advanced techniques for influence and persuasion but also carries significant ethical responsibility. "Nudges" and other behavioral interventions can be powerful tools to guide decisions toward more rational and beneficial behavior, but their implementation must be handled carefully.

Ethics in this field refers to the need to respect individuals' autonomy, avoiding manipulations that could lead to harmful or unfair decisions. Furthermore, the responsibility in designing these strategies includes the obligation to ensure that interventions are transparent, fair, and aligned with the best interests of the participants. In this regard, it becomes crucial to create a balance between the effectiveness of strategies and respect for the rights and well-being of users.

1. The Line Between Persuasion and Manipulation

Ethical Context: Behavioral finance tools, such as nudges, can benefit investors if designed to guide them toward optimal decisions, but there is also the risk of manipulation.

Problematic Cases:

"Guaranteed returns" offers exploiting the availability heuristic.

Trading platforms that gamify the experience, promoting overtrading.

Recommendation: Transparency in the strategy design objectives and regulation to ensure that the client's interests are prioritized.

The design of behavioral strategies must be carefully considered to avoid crossing the line between persuasion and manipulation. While nudges can be effective in guiding investors toward more informed and rational decisions, it is essential to ensure that individuals' cognitive vulnerabilities are not exploited. To achieve this, strategy designers must maintain a transparent approach, clearly communicating the objectives and benefits of interventions, and implementing regulations that protect users' interests. This way, a transparent environment is promoted where ethical persuasion helps individuals without sacrificing their autonomy or integrity.

2. Automated Decisions and Implicit Biases in AI

- **Key Risks**:

AI algorithms can perpetuate biases if the historical data used is biased.

Automated decisions that prioritize business benefits over the financial well-being of the user.

- **Example**: An automated investment platform could suggest higher-commission products instead of those better suited to the client's profile.
- **Solution**:

Regular audits of AI models.

Incorporation of ethical principles in algorithmic design, ensuring neutrality and fairness.

Automated decisions, especially those driven by AI, present a significant ethical and fairness challenge. The presence of implicit biases in algorithms can distort results and jeopardize users' well-being by favoring business interests over financial ones. To mitigate these risks, it is essential for automated investment platforms to undergo regular audits and for ethical principles to be incorporated into algorithm design. Only in this way can AI systems operate neutrally and fairly, benefiting investors without hidden biases.

3. The Responsibility of Market Actors

- **Key Actors**:

Companies: Design responsible financial products that do not exploit cognitive vulnerabilities.

Investors: Educate themselves to make informed decisions and not rely entirely on technological tools.

Regulators: Create a regulatory framework that promotes transparency and protects investors.

- **Practical Example**: Clear disclosure requirements on digital platforms about how user data is used to design financial strategies or nudges.

The responsibility for designing and managing behavioral strategies lies not only with regulators but also with companies and investors. Companies must develop financial products that respect individuals' autonomy, avoiding tactics that exploit cognitive biases. Investors, for their part, must continually educate themselves to make informed decisions and not rely entirely on technological tools. Regulators have an essential role in creating frameworks that foster transparency and protect investors. This collaborative approach among all actors ensures a fairer and more equitable market for all involved.

4. Proactive Regulation in Emerging Markets

- **Specific Challenges**:

Markets with high volatility and lower levels of financial education.

Risk of vulnerable investors falling into fraudulent schemes.

- **Regulatory Proposals**:

Create minimum standards for AI-based and behavioral finance tools.

Establish sanctions for companies promoting abusive practices.

Emerging markets face unique challenges due to their high volatility and relatively low levels of financial education. These factors can lead vulnerable investors to fall into fraudulent schemes or make uninformed decisions. To counter these issues, it is vital to implement proactive regulations that include clear standards for AI-based and behavioral finance tools. By establishing sanctions for companies that promote abusive practices, a safer and more transparent investment environment can be ensured in these emerging markets.

Recommendations for Practitioners and Educators

In the context of behavioral finance and the use of technological tools, both practitioners and educators play a fundamental role in shaping a more ethical and efficient market. For professionals designing strategies and financial products, it is essential to consider the emotional and cognitive impacts on investors, seeking not only to maximize returns but also to foster more rational and responsible decision-making.

On the other hand, educators must lead the transmission of this knowledge, helping future professionals understand the principles of behavioral economics and the ethical implications of emerging technologies. In this way, both practitioners and educators contribute to creating a more transparent, responsible, and aware ecosystem of the cognitive needs and limitations of investors.

A. How to Teach Behavioral Finance in the Classroom

1. **Integration of Theory and Practice:**

Real-life Examples: Use historical and current case studies, such as the dot-com bubble or the subprime crisis, to illustrate how behavioral biases affect markets.

Interactive Simulations: Incorporate investment simulation platforms where students can experience the consequences of their decisions, allowing them to see in real time how emotions and biases influence their outcomes.

2. **Development of Critical Thinking Skills:**

Debates and Discussions: Encourage the analysis of financial situations from different perspectives, seeking to identify possible biases and how they alter rational decisions.

Reflection Techniques: Ask students to reflect on their personal financial decisions, helping them identify biases in their behavior and improve their decision-making skills.

3. **Use of Innovative Technologies:**

Digital Tools: Leverage big data, artificial intelligence, and market sentiment analysis to help students understand how systems can be used to analyze behavioral patterns and make predictions.

4. **Promotion of Interdisciplinarity:**

Connection with Psychology and Neuroscience: Introduce concepts from other disciplines, such as cognitive psychology and neuroeconomics, to provide a more comprehensive perspective on how individuals make financial decisions.

The practical approach and integration of various perspectives, such as using real cases, interactive simulations, and digital tools, are essential for students to understand the complexities of behavioral finance. Through these learning experiences, students can develop critical skills to identify and manage emotional and cognitive biases affecting financial decisions, both in markets and in their personal lives. This training not only prepares students to face the challenges of today's financial world but also makes them more informed and responsible decision-makers in the future.

B. Methods for Implementing These Strategies in Financial Companies

1. **Continuous Training for Employees:**

Behavioral Training Programs: Develop programs that educate employees on how cognitive biases can affect investment decisions, and teach them how to avoid impulsive or irrational decisions in their interactions with clients.

Training in Data-Driven Decision Making: Train employees to use data analysis tools and predictive algorithms, helping them make more informed decisions based on market behaviors and patterns.

2. **Designing Responsible Financial Products:**

Customer-Centered Approach: Ensure that financial products and services are designed with consumer well-being in mind, avoiding marketing practices that exploit biases like loss aversion or overconfidence.

Use of Ethical Nudges: Implement nudges that guide consumers toward more beneficial financial decisions without coercing them, such as recommending saving more or investing more diversely.

3. **Real-Time Behavior Analysis:**

Big Data and Sentiment Analysis: Implement tools that analyze market sentiment and investor behavior, allowing real-time adjustments to sales and communication strategies.

Tracking Decisions and Adjustments: Monitor client decisions on investment platforms to identify potential biases and provide real-time feedback to help them make more rational decisions.

4. **Organizational Culture Aware of Biases:**

Promote Reflection on Internal Biases: Foster an organizational culture where internal biases within teams are recognized, helping employees become more aware of their influence on the decision-making process.

Encourage Interdisciplinary Collaboration: Integrate teams that combine knowledge in finance, psychology, neuroscience, and technology to create more complete and ethical financial products.

Implementing behavioral strategies in financial companies not only improves internal decision-making but also helps create more responsible products and fosters a culture of awareness of biases. Training employees, designing products centered on consumer well-being, and leveraging real-time data analysis enables companies to optimize their processes and offer solutions more aligned with the real needs of consumers. The integration of these methods not only benefits clients but also promotes an ethical and sustainable approach within the organization, key to long-term success.

Conclusion: Behavioral Finance in Action

The integration of behavioral concepts into finance has moved from being a mere academic curiosity to becoming a powerful tool in real-world decision-making. Well-designed behavioral strategies can transform the way investors, companies, and governments address the challenges of modern markets. Key takeaways include:

Evolution Toward a More Human Approach: Recognizing emotions and biases not only allows for better prediction of market movements but also helps design solutions more aligned with people's needs.

Simulation and Analysis: The New Educational and Professional Standard: Practical simulations have proven essential for understanding the psychological mechanisms that shape decisions under pressure, vital learning for both individuals and organizations.

The Central Role of Ethics: In a world where technological tools amplify the ability to influence decisions, financial actors have an inescapable responsibility: to create a fair, transparent system oriented toward the general well-being.

Toward the Future: Behavioral finance not only explains the past or interprets the present; it also shapes the future. With the advent of technologies like artificial intelligence, personalization, and big data analysis, the possibilities for innovation are endless. However, the real challenge will be to find a balance between economic benefits and social impact.

CONCLUSION

Final Reflections and the Role of Behavior in the Finance of Tomorrow

The journey we have undertaken throughout this book reveals how the interplay between psychology, technology, and financial markets has transformed our understanding of economics. From traditional finance, rooted in assumptions of rationality and efficiency, to behavioral finance, which embraces human complexity and imperfections, each stage has added depth to how we analyze financial decisions.

Human Behavior at the Core of Transformation

Human behavior lies at the heart of this transformation. Cognitive and emotional biases, once ignored or minimized, have become central elements in understanding phenomena such as market bubbles, financial crises, and investment dynamics. We have learned that economic decisions are not solely influenced by data and rational theories but also by emotions, perceptions, and collective narratives.

A Future Driven by Technology and Behavior

Looking ahead, tomorrow's finance will increasingly be defined by technology. Artificial intelligence (AI), big data, and predictive models promise an era of unprecedented personalization and precision. However, this technological progress will not replace the importance of the human factor; instead, it will complement and, in some cases, amplify it.

- **The role of AI and behavioral finance:** As AI becomes a core tool for designing financial strategies, the challenge will be ensuring these technologies uphold ethics and promote responsible decision-making. Emotional algorithms, for instance, have the potential to empower investors by correcting biases and encouraging better decisions but could also be used to manipulate behavior if not adequately monitored.

- **The rise of cognitive-behavioral finance:** The integration of neuroscience, psychology, and AI promises to inaugurate a new paradigm in which financial systems not only predict but also influence human behavior. This approach could revolutionize financial education, investment strategies, and market regulation.

The Role of Behavior in a Complex World

In a global environment marked by uncertainty, financial markets will continue to reflect the emotions and narratives of individuals and societies. The concepts explored in this book remind us that understanding human behavior is essential not only to predict the future but also to design it. Behavioral finance has shown that the market is not a perfect machine; it is a living organism driven by the decisions of millions of people, each with their own aspirations, fears, and expectations.

The future of finance requires a balanced approach that combines technological innovation with a deep understanding of human behavior. This balance will not only help create more efficient and equitable markets but also address global challenges—from economic inequality to climate change—with more human and sustainable solutions.

Closing Thoughts: A Call for Reflection

I invite readers to take these ideas beyond the pages of this book. Finance is not a static field; it is a mirror of our ever-evolving humanity. Understanding it means better understanding ourselves—our biases, strengths, and vulnerabilities. Here lies the true power of behavioral finance: in its ability to connect the rigor of economics with the complexity of human behavior and in its potential to inspire positive change in markets and in our lives.

APPENDICES

Glossary of Key Terms

1. **Market Anomalies**:
   Deviations in financial asset prices from levels predicted by traditional financial theory. These anomalies can result from irrational investor behaviors, such as overconfidence or overreaction to information.
2. **Fundamental Analysis**:
   An approach that evaluates an asset's intrinsic value by considering economic, financial, and other relevant factors. It contrasts with technical analysis, which focuses on past price movements.
3. **Technical Analysis**:
   A method for evaluating financial securities based on market statistics, mainly price and volume data, to predict future price movements.
4. **Financial Bubbles**:
   Periods where financial asset prices inflate to unsustainable levels due to widespread speculation, followed by sudden collapses. Historical examples include the dot-com bubble and the subprime mortgage crisis.
5. **Investor Behavior**:
   The study of decisions and actions by individuals investing in financial markets, influenced by psychological, emotional, and cognitive factors rather than purely rational decision-making.
6. **Overconfidence**:
   A cognitive bias where investors overestimate their ability to predict the market, leading to excessively risky decisions due to a false sense of control or knowledge.

7. **Market Efficiency**:
   A theory asserting that asset prices reflect all available information, making it impossible to consistently achieve superior returns without taking on more risk.

8. **Emotions and Finance**:
   The impact of human emotions, such as fear, greed, and euphoria, on investment decisions and market behavior. This concept is central to behavioral finance.

9. **Irrational Exuberance**:
   A term coined by Robert Shiller to describe impulsive investor actions driven by euphoria, creating asset bubbles that eventually burst.

10. **Heuristics**:
    Mental shortcuts or general rules used for quick decision-making, especially under uncertainty. While often useful, they can lead to systematic judgment errors.

11. **Rational Expectations Hypothesis (REH)**:
    An economic theory suggesting that economic agents make fully rational decisions using all available information and accurately anticipate future conditions.

12. **Efficient Market Hypothesis (EMH)**:
    A theory positing that financial asset prices always reflect all available information, implying that extraordinary returns cannot be consistently achieved without additional risk.

13. **Emotion-Driven Investing**:
    The tendency of investors to make decisions based on feelings like fear, anxiety, or optimism, rather than performing rational, logical market analysis.

14. **Bounded Rationality**:

A concept proposed by Herbert Simon, suggesting that decision-making is limited by available information, time constraints, and cognitive processing capacity.

15. **Investor Sentiment**:
General attitudes, emotions, and expectations of investors influencing asset prices. Often irrational, it can deviate from fundamental valuations.

16. **Cognitive Biases**:
Systematic judgment errors caused by the way the brain processes information. These biases influence economic decision-making, such as overestimating probabilities or misinterpreting data.

17. **Confirmation Bias**:
The tendency to seek, interpret, and remember information that confirms preexisting beliefs, while ignoring or discounting contradictory evidence.

18. **Prospect Theory**:
Developed by Kahneman and Tversky, this theory describes how people make decisions under risk and uncertainty, showing that losses weigh more heavily than equivalent gains, leading to behaviors like loss aversion.

19. **Efficient Market Hypothesis (EMH)**:
Proposed by Eugene Fama, this theory holds that financial asset prices reflect all available information, meaning investors cannot consistently outperform the market without assuming more risk.

20. **Anchoring Bias**:
A cognitive bias where individuals rely too heavily on the first piece of information (the "anchor") when making decisions, even if it is irrelevant or incorrect.

21. **Asset Valuation**:

The process of determining the intrinsic value of an asset, such as a stock or bond, using various methodologies that consider economic, financial, and market factors.

22. **Overreaction and Underreaction**:
Market phenomena where investors tend to overreact to recent news (creating bubbles) or underreact to significant events (causing inefficiencies).

23. **Loss Aversion Paradox**:
A psychological theory suggesting that people feel the pain of a loss much more intensely than the pleasure of an equivalent gain. This phenomenon influences financial and investment decisions.

24. **Adaptive Market Hypothesis**:
Proposed by Andrew Lo, it suggests that markets are neither completely efficient nor entirely inefficient but are adaptive, with participants evolving and learning from experience and changing conditions.

25. **Sentiment Analysis**:
A technique that uses qualitative data, such as social media posts or news, to measure market emotions and attitudes toward a financial asset or economic topic.

26. **Behavioral Alpha**:
Additional value that portfolio managers can generate by incorporating behavioral finance principles into their investment strategies.

27. **Big Data**:
Massive sets of structured and unstructured data analyzed to identify patterns, trends, and correlations in financial markets.

28. **Bias**:
A systematic tendency to make judgment errors or decisions due to cognitive or emotional factors.

29. **Blockchain**:
    A distributed ledger technology ensuring digital transactions' security through cryptography, mainly used in cryptocurrencies and financial applications.

30. **Cryptocurrency**:
    A digital asset that uses blockchain technology to ensure secure and decentralized transactions. Examples include Bitcoin and Ethereum.

31. **Automated Decisions**:
    Resolutions made by artificial intelligence systems without direct human intervention, based on algorithms and historical data.

32. **Nudge Design**:
    Behavioral strategies designed to influence individuals' decisions without limiting their freedom of choice, applied in finance to encourage behaviors like saving.

33. **Irrational Exuberance**:
    A term popularized by Robert Shiller describing asset overvaluation driven by collective emotions and behaviors in markets.

34. **Cognitive Finance**:
    An emerging field combining neuroscience and economics to understand how brain processes impact financial decisions.

35. **Efficient Market Hypothesis (EMH)**:
    A theory stating that asset prices reflect all available information, making it impossible to consistently achieve higher-than-average returns without additional risk.

36. **Investor Sentiment Indexes**:
    Tools that quantify market emotions and perceptions, used to predict trends and potential price shifts.

37. **Neuroeconomics**:
   A discipline studying the interaction between brain processes and economic decision-making, combining psychology, neuroscience, and economics.

38. **Nudge**:
   An intervention in the decision environment that promotes desired behaviors without relying on financial incentives or restrictions.

39. **Overconfidence**:
   A bias where investors overestimate their knowledge, skills, or ability to predict the market, potentially leading to risky decisions.

40. **Prospect Theory**:
   A model developed by Kahneman and Tversky describing how people make risky decisions, disproportionately weighing perceived gains and losses.

41. **Bounded Rationality**:
   Herbert Simon's concept indicating that human decisions are constrained by cognitive limitations, time, and information availability.

42. **Confirmation Bias**:
   The tendency to seek, interpret, and remember information in a way that confirms preexisting beliefs, ignoring contradictory evidence.

43. **Anchoring Bias**:
   The influence of an initial value ("anchor") on subsequent estimates or decisions, even if the anchor is irrelevant.

44. **Asset Tokenization**:
   The process of representing physical or financial assets as digital tokens on a blockchain, enabling greater liquidity and divisibility.

45. **Volatility**:
A measure of the variability or instability in a financial asset's price over a specific period.

46. **WealthTech**:
Financial technology focused on wealth management, using artificial intelligence and big data to personalize investment strategies.

47. **Behavioral Bias**:
Systematic errors in financial decision-making stemming from emotions or irrational thought patterns.

48. **Sentiment Analysis**:
Using AI tools to assess the emotional tone of financial texts, such as news or social media, and measure their market impact.

49. **Herding**:
The tendency of investors to follow others' decisions, creating massive market movements without solid economic fundamentals.

Bibliography and Recommended Resources

1. Acemoglu, D., & Restrepo, P. (2019). Artificial Intelligence, Automation, and Work. Econometrica, 88(6), 2195–2223.

2. Agrawal, A., Gans, J., & Goldfarb, A. (2018). Prediction Machines: The Simple Economics of Artificial Intelligence. Harvard Business Review Press.

3. Akerlof, G. A., & Shiller, R. J. (2009). *Animal Spirits: How Human Psychology Drives the Economy, and Why It Matters for Global Capitalism*. Princeton University Press.

4. Baker, M., & Wurgler, J. (2006). Investor Sentiment and the Cross-Section of Stock Returns. Journal of Finance, 61(4), 1645–1680.

5. Baker, M., & Wurgler, J. (2007). *Investor Sentiment in the Stock Market*. Journal of Economic Perspectives, 21(2), 129-152.

6. Barberis, N., & Thaler, R. (2003). *A Survey of Behavioral Finance. Handbook of the Economics of Finance*, 1, 1053-1128.

7. Barberis, N., Shleifer, A., & Vishny, R. W. (1998). *A Model of Investor Sentiment. Journal of Financial Economics, 49*(3), 307-343.

8. Benartzi, S., & Thaler, R. H. (1995). *Myopic Loss Aversion and the Equity Premium Puzzle. Quarterly Journal of Economics, 110*(1), 73-92.

9. Black, F., & Scholes, M. (1973). *The Pricing of Options and Corporate Liabilities. Journal of Political Economy, 81*(3), 637-654.

10. Bollen, J., Mao, H., & Zeng, X. (2011). Twitter Mood Predicts the Stock Market. Journal of Computational Science, 2(1), 1–8.

11. Brogaard, J., Hendershott, T., & Riordan, R. (2014). High-Frequency Trading and Price Discovery. Review of Financial Studies, 27(8), 2267–2306.

12. Challet, D., Marsili, M., & Zhang, Y. C. (2005). Minority Games: Interacting Agents in Financial Markets. Oxford University Press.

13. Chen, H., De, P., Hu, Y., & Hwang, B. H. (2014). Wisdom of Crowds: The Value of Stock Opinions Transmitted Through Social Media. Review of Financial Studies, 27(5), 1367–1403.

14. Daniel, K., & Titman, S. (1997). Evidence on the Characteristics of Cross-Sectional Variation in Stock Returns. Journal of Finance, 52(1), 1–33.

15. Das, S. R. (2014). Text and Context: Language Analytics in Finance. Foundations and Trends in Finance, 8(3), 145–261.

16. De Bondt, W. F., & Thaler, R. H. (1985). *Does the Stock Market Overreact?. Journal of Finance, 40*(3), 793-805.

17. Fama, E. F. (1970). *Efficient Capital Markets: A Review of Theory and Empirical Work. Journal of Finance, 25*(2), 383-417.

18. Fama, E. F., & French, K. R. (1993). *Common Risk Factors in the Returns on Stocks and Bonds. Journal of Financial Economics, 33*(1), 3-56.

19. Gennaioli, N., Shleifer, A., & Vishny, R. (2015). *Money Doctors. Journal of Finance, 70*(1), 91-114.

20. Gennaioli, N., Shleifer, A., & Vishny, R. W. (2015). Neglected Risks: The Psychology of Financial Crises. Journal of Financial Economics, 115(3), 471–492.

21. Goodell, J. W., & Goutte, S. (2021). Co-Movement of COVID-19 and Bitcoin: Evidence from Wavelet Coherence Analysis. Finance Research Letters, 38, 101625.

22. Hirshleifer, D. (2001). *Investor Psychology and Asset Pricing. Journal of Finance, 56*(4), 1533-1597.

23. Hirshleifer, D. (2001). Investor Psychology and Asset Pricing. Journal of Finance, 56(4), 1533–1597.

24. Kahneman, D. (2011). *Thinking, Fast and Slow*. Farrar, Straus and Giroux.

25. Kahneman, D., & Tversky, A. (1979). Prospect Theory: An Analysis of Decision under Risk. Econometrica, 47(2), 263–291.

26. Kearney, C., & Liu, S. (2014). Textual Sentiment in Finance: A Survey of Methods and Models. International Review of Financial Analysis, 33, 171–185.

27. Kindleberger, C. P., & Aliber, R. Z. (2011). *Manias, Panics, and Crashes: A History of Financial Crises*. Palgrave Macmillan.

28. King, G. & Lowe, W. (2003). Analyzing Sentences to Extract Information: Computerized Methods for Extracting Knowledge from Text. American Political Science Review, 97(2), 221–236.

29. Langer, E. J. (1975). *The Illusion of Control. Journal of Personality and Social Psychology, 32*(2), 311-328.

30. Laza, S. (2019). *Neuroeconomía: La Nueva Ciencia de las Decisiones*. Editorial Libryco.

31. Laza, S., & Cuevas Sarmiento, M. (2021). *Economía de las Emociones*. Editorial Libryco.

32. Lo, A. W. (2004). *The Adaptive Markets Hypothesis: Market Efficiency from an Evolutionary Perspective. Journal of Portfolio Management, 30*(5), 15-29.

33. Lo, A. W. (2004). The Adaptive Markets Hypothesis: Market Efficiency from an Evolutionary Perspective. Journal of Portfolio Management, 30(5), 15–29.

34. Malkiel, B. G. (1999). *A Random Walk Down Wall Street*. W. W. Norton & Company.

35. Mayer-Schönberger, V., & Cukier, K. (2013). Big Data: A Revolution That Will Transform How We Live, Work, and Think. Houghton Mifflin Harcourt.

36. Preis, T., Moat, H. S., & Stanley, H. E. (2013). Quantifying Trading Behavior in Financial Markets Using Google Trends. Scientific Reports, 3(1), 1684.

37. Shefrin, H. (2000). *Beyond Greed and Fear: Understanding Behavioral Finance and the Psychology of Investing*. Oxford University Press.

38. Shiller, R. J. (2000). Irrational Exuberance. Princeton University Press.

39. Tetlock, P. C. (2007). *Giving Content to Investor Sentiment: The Role of Media in the Stock Market. Journal of Finance, 62*(3), 1139-1168.

40. Tetlock, P. C. (2007). Giving Content to Investor Sentiment: The Role of Media in the Stock Market. Journal of Finance, 62(3), 1139–1168.

41. Tetlock, P. C., Saar-Tsechansky, M., & Macskassy, S. (2008). More than Words: Quantifying Language to Measure Firms' Fundamentals. Journal of Finance, 63(3), 1437–1467.

42. Thaler, R. H. (2015). *Misbehaving: The Making of Behavioral Economics.* W. W. Norton & Company.

43. Thaler, R., & Sunstein, C. R. (2008). Nudge: Improving Decisions About Health, Wealth, and Happiness. Yale University Press.

44. Tversky, A., & Kahneman, D. (1974). *Judgment under Uncertainty: Heuristics and Biases. Science, 185*(4157), 1124-1131.

45. Tversky, A., & Kahneman, D. (1981). *The Framing of Decisions and the Psychology of Choice. Science, 211*(4481), 453-458.

46. Zervoudakis, K., & Griffin, C. (2016). Sentiment Analysis in Finance: Current Trends and Future Directions. Financial Innovation, 2(1), 23–35.

www.ingramcontent.com/pod-product-compliance
Lightning Source LLC
Chambersburg PA
CBHW071054240526
45471CB00015B/1865